The Social Economy
of the Tlingit Indians

KALERVO OBERG

Foreword by Wilson Duff

UNIVERSITY OF WASHINGTON PRESS
Seattle and London

Library of Congress Cataloging in Publication Data
Oberg, Kalervo, 1901–1973.
    The social economy of the Tlingit Indians.

    (American Ethnological Society. Monograph 55)
    Bibliography: p.
    1. Tlingit Indians—Economic conditions.
I. Title. II. Series.
E99.T603 1973   330.9'701   73-16048
ISBN 0-295-95290-3

Chapter opening ornaments after George Emmons, *The Basketry of the Tlinkit* (1903)

FOREWORD

There is more than one ironic twist in the circumstances that result in the publication in 1973 of the splendid study of Tlingit economic and social life which Kalervo Oberg completed in 1933. Not the least poignant of these is that the author did not live to see his doctoral dissertation finally published, although he was attending to details of its preparation before his death early this summer. But what is to be regretted most is that the study has lain unnoticed for so long, virtually ignored by two generations of Northwest Coast scholars, when it should have its rightful place in the debates which have ebbed and flowed over that time. It is a cornerstone placed late, and an example of the curiously uncoordinated manner in which the ethnographic literature on the Tlingit, which we suddenly realize is now substantial indeed, has grown. And it seems to me that this posthumous publication is a fitting marker to the end of an era, the era of university-initiated ethnographic research on the Northwest Coast. I think we are into a time of changing initiatives and new directions of inquiry, and also into a time when academic anthropology will be called into account by the people it has presumed to describe for the manner in which it has interpreted their cultures. Oberg's study has already been subjected to a brief skirmish with a Tlingit view of things, as I shall recount briefly below, and the episode has provided one opportunity to look at the validities of both sides of the case, and see the abiding strengths, if also some of the weaknesses, of one example of academic anthropology on the Northwest Coast.

The literature on the Tlingit has grown in a strangely uneven way since the early, museum-oriented studies of Emmons and Swanton, and of Krause. Apart from the unique contributions of the tragically ambivalent and controversial Tlingit nobleman Louis Shotridge, and the considerable body of sound data which came to be incorporated into the legal and semi-legal documents involved with land claims litigation, it has come predominantly from the hands of university-based anthropologists. Kalervo Oberg from Chicago in 1931 was the first of these, followed soon by Ronald Olson and Philip Drucker from California, Erna Gunther and Viola Garfield from Washington, and more recently Frederica de Laguna from Bryn Mawr and Catherine McClellan from Wisconsin. The publications of these scholars now form a substantial literature. But they seem to have shown a curious disregard for each others' work. For example, Olson's "Social Structure and Social Life of the Tlingit in Alaska," based on field work between 1933 and 1954, made a belated and unobtrusive appearance in 1967, and is a solid but isolated piece of scholarly description. And de Laguna's encyclopedic 3-volume monograph on the Yakutat appeared in 1972, but with no mention of either Oberg or Olson in the bibliography. Each, however, has made its own distinctive contribution, and none of the others duplicate the task which Oberg set for himself.

Of all the writers on the Tlingit, the only one who mentions this study of Oberg's is Wendell Oswalt, who consulted it for his chapter on the Tlingit in *This Land Was Theirs* (New York: Wiley, 1966). He was moved to comment that "Oberg's discussions of the social system and economy are outstanding for their clarity and breadth; and it is little short of amazing that this work has never been published" (p. 343). I heartily agree. One would have thought that Oberg's 1937 article on "Crime and Punishment in Tlingit Society" in the *American Anthropologist* would have whetted the appetite for more, but obviously it did not.

I mentioned above that we are into a time of changing initiatives and new directions of inquiry, and nearing the end of the period of university-initiated field research. One of the new directions, I am sure, will be back to the museums and the older literature for a more perceptive look at art, myth, and other expressive aspects of culture. Much of the philosophy and metaphysics of the Northwest Coast still resides there, waiting to be read by the perceptive eye of structural analysis. But the major change, I predict, will be a shift in the locus of field research from the universities to the people themselves. The topics, phrasings, and interpretations will increasingly be their own. Along with this will come an examination and testing of the previous work of anthropologists; not just of their ethnographic descriptions, but also of the concepts which they, as expert witnesses in court cases, have helped to harden into law.

An example of such testing was provided by comments on *The Social Economy of the Tlingit Indians* offered by William L. Paul, Sr., the distinguished Tlingit lawyer and Grand President Emeritus of the Alaska Native Brotherhood. Mr. Paul had heard of the author, for Oberg had testified in certain of the land cases. In fact Mr. Paul, unlike most anthropologists, had long since read Oberg's dissertation and formed definite opinions about it. The following comments are based on a reading of a memorandum written by Mr. Paul.

One of Mr. Paul's strongly stated and all too valid criticisms of the writings of anthropologists on the Tlingit (and he has read them all), is concerned with the description of Tlinget concepts by other than Tlingit words. He points out that such words as "chief," "tribe," "phratry," "potlatch," "sacred," fail to convey exact Tlingit meanings and inevitably carry with them extraneous meanings which are not acceptable to the Tlingit. It is a problem that anthropologists recognize all too well, and one which we can never fully solve while we write about other cultures in English, the language of our own. But sometimes we contribute unnecessarily to the confusion. I think there is unnecessary redundancy, for example, in our use of the words "clan," "phratry," and "moiety" in describing Tlingit culture. "Clan" could probably be made to serve the purpose alone, with "sub-clan" for the autonomous local subdivisions. (Mr. Paul would prefer to use the word "tribe" for the latter. He describes himself as "a member of the Teehitton tribe of the Raven clan.")

"Chief," to Mr. Paul, is a word "transplanted from the lower 48" which carries meanings inapplicable to Tlingit society. It would be better if everybody were to learn and use the proper Tlingit terms, which Oberg gives as *yitsati* (housekeeper) and *ankaua* (rich man), and Mr. Paul gives as *hit-zahty* (house master) and *ahn-kah-woo*. Mr. Paul's criticisms in this case are not directed particularly at Oberg, who does use the Tlingit terms, and acknowledges that "the word chief does not fit the *ankaua* any more than it does the *yitsati*." They are directed at general English usage, and take their force from well-remembered attempts to clarify the concepts in court. His comments do, however, help to sharpen our understanding of the two terms. The *hit-zahty* was "master" of the house in everything, and might be a war leader as well, depending on his abilities. The role of *ahn-kah-woo* was not something that one could inherit. It was given by consensus, "like the 33rd honorary degree of the Masons." Furthermore, the presence of only two *ahn-kah-woo* in any town was accidental, as it was a title that could go to anybody who became rich enough and gave the right number of feasts. Oberg's term "*ankaua*-ship" should perhaps be read as having an element of "*ankaua*-tude" in it.

This problem of words is not just a matter of tidy description. Court proceedings, like anthropological debates, are conducted in English. In testifying as expert witnesses, anthropologists are playing a very serious game that deeply affects the lives and fortunes of the people they represent, and had better know the limits of their expertise. Mr. Paul accuses one such witness of having testified that the Tlingit "had so little conception of land as property that they had no word for land," when the fact is that there are three such words. The stakes in that game were terribly high. Anthropologists have also testified on the use of the word "tribe" as it applies to the Tlingit. In their minds it best applies to the "-quan," or localized federations of sub-clans (for example, the Stikine-quan or Stikine tribe, comprised of nine sub-clans). On the strength of that, the U.S. Court of Claims has created the legal fiction that the Tlingit consist of fourteen "tribes." This does violence to the Tlingit view of the situation as expressed by Mr. Paul. To him, the fundamental and autonomous political divisions of Tlingit society are the sub-clans, and it is for these that he would reserve the word "tribe." It is not just a pointless debate over one or other use of a word, for in the process a concept repugnant to the Tlingit has become hardened into law.

Mr. Paul's comments help to clear up several other points which have not been well understood by anthropologists. One of these is the proper identity of the puzzling third clan of the Tongass Tlingit, the Nexadi. The basic fact is that there are only two Tlingit clans, one headed by the Raven emblem and the other by the Wolf. The Nexadi are of the Raven clan. It is true that they use the Eagle as an emblem, but then so do the Haida Eagles, who as the Tlingit understand are really Ravens as well!

The reason why the Tlingit Raven clan is called Tlaienadi (Paul: *hlei-nadi* "all on one side") is that in this clan the Raven does not share its unique position with any other emblem, while on the opposite side the Bear, Killer Whale, and Eagle hold equal rank as emblems with the Wolf. The name "Tlingit" itself, as Mr. Paul explains it, is not a Tlingit but a Tsimshian name—a contraction of a phrase which means "from-place-of-tidal-waters-people."

However it is not my purpose here to glean all possible information from his comments. For the greater part they confirm, rephrase and supplement what Oberg has to say. There are two points of disagreement, however, which I think should be mentioned. Oberg writes that there were two crimes that called for the death penalty: witchcraft and incest (page 41). Mr. Paul explains that there were ways of escaping that penalty in both cases. In the case of witchcraft, it was by confession; and in the case of incest, by voluntarily submitting to ostracism until such time as one could accumulate enough wealth to give a great feast. In both cases however the taint of the crime was never forgotten. According to Oberg, control over the trade routes to the interior was claimed by the Kagwantan of Klukwan, but Mr. Paul comments: "This was only the self-praise of Oberg's Klukwan informant. When the British built a fort at Selkirk and interfered with the trade of the Klukwan, it was the Gahn-nuxuddy who raided the fort over 300 miles north, not the Kagwantan."

I think it most significant that none of Mr. Paul's comments are directed at the central core and substance of Oberg's study, that is, at the "rather specific problems" of the workings of the traditional economic and social system which he set out to explore. These are matters of anthropological interest which are not perhaps of much conscious concern to a member of the society. Mr. Paul's main concerns are with the fullness and accuracy of the ethnographic and historical facts.

Oberg was not writing an ethnography in the ordinary sense, though he gives a great deal of ethnographic information. Indeed his analysis of such aspects of the culture as marriage preferences, kinship, and the potlatch show his understanding of the proper phrasings of the social and religious aspects of Tlingit life and his deep penetration into Tlingit thought. However, Oberg's ethnographic information is always given in the context of its controlling ideas and principles—the inner workings and dynamic balancing of the system—and there is where the abiding strength and worth of his study lies.

Wilson Duff
Vancouver, B.C.
August 1973

PREFACE

Toward the end of the 1920s there were lively discussions between the economists and anthropologists at the University of Chicago concerning economic behavior in tribal societies. These debates were led by Dr. F. H. Knight of the economics department and Dr. Edward Sapir of the anthropology department. The economists wanted to know what forces governed the distribution of goods and services and what determined exchange values in an economy with no organized markets and no money. The anthropologists pointed out that distributive transactions were governed by tribal custom and that values were also culturally determined. Further discussion disclosed that while this was so, values nevertheless were not static but, over a period of time, some change was characteristic in exchange values. The economists were interested in these changes and wanted to know in detail what influences brought about change.

At the time I was a graduate student in economics at the University of Pittsburgh. During the year I became acquainted with Mr. Homer Jones, an instructor in economics and a former student of Dr. Knight. When he learned that I had been brought up on the Northwest Coast and had a general knowledge of the Indians, particularly of their potlatch, and was writing my master's thesis on the history of the theory of value in economics, he wrote Dr. Knight that I might be useful to either him or Dr. Sapir in their effort to clarify their differences concerning tribal economics. Dr. Knight was very much interested but indicated that he had already committed all his fellowship funds for the coming year. He added, however, that Dr. Sapir was willing to have me come to Chicago for a year and then go into the field to make a study of the economy of some Indian tribe. The following September (1930) found me in Chicago. While taking courses in anthropology and reading as much as possible, I discussed with Sapir the choice of the tribe to be studied. Sapir pointed out that as I had some acquaintance with the Northwest and that as wealth was important among the Northwest tribes, that would be the logical area for research. As considerable information already existed concerning the Kwakiutl, Haida, and Tsimshian, he suggested that it would be rewarding to make a study of the less known Tlingit of southeastern Alaska. I then read all available material on the Tlingit, particularly the works of Franz Boas and John R. Swanton. The above authors concentrated on collecting Tlingit texts, and, although there was no systematic approach to the economy of the Tlingit, there was considerable material on social organization, the potlatch, and myths, which gave a general picture of Tlingit culture. The research of Aurel Krause, a German geographer in the 1880s, was published in Jena in 1885, under the title, *Die Tlingit Indianer.* (This work is considered to be the best account of the Tlingit, and was translated by Erna Gunther and published in 1955 by the University of Washington Press.)

In June 1931, I arrived in Juneau, Alaska. It soon became apparent that there was pronounced tension between the whites and the Indians. I received no encouragement from the white residents. The Indians on the outskirts of Juneau were mostly young people working at various jobs for the whites. When I questioned them as to life in their villages, I was met with blank stares or statements to the effect that they did not know much about the old ways of the Tlingit. At a Chamber of Commerce meeting which I attended, I was told that the Indians were a "lazy bunch of bums." However, one member of the group told me that I should meet Father Kashaveroff of the Alaska Museum, who was well informed about the Tlingit Indians. I called on Kashaveroff and was much encouraged by his enthusiasm and kindness. He informed me that the best place to begin my research was Klukwan, about twenty-three miles up the Chilkat River from Haines. This village, he claimed, was the least influenced by the whites; then I should study the Indians in Sitka and Wrangell. He gave me the names of old men and women in each of these villages who, he said, were well informed about the past and who would be cooperative.

After spending some time reading the books in the museum and making trips to small Tlingit settlements near Juneau, I embarked in August on a steamer for Haines at the mouth of the Chilkat River. It took me a couple of weeks to plan out my trip to Klukwan. I had to find a place to live. Eventually the Alaska Road Commission allowed me to use their summer camp three miles above Klukwan. This was a large log cabin equipped with stoves and beds.

As I planned to winter here, there were a number of things I had to do. First I had to cut firewood and partition off a part of the large log cabin. This I did by salvaging planks from a broken down building which had been a store at one time. I then lined the room with heavy building paper. Before the snow came in October, there were trucks passing by supplying a prospecters' camp at Forty Mile Post on the Yukon border. My nearest white neighbor lived at Thirty Mile Post. He was very helpful as he knew the country well.

Late in October I went to Haines for supplies. I bought half a hog, a quarter of a reindeer, fifty pounds of beef, beans, rice, bacon, and a reserve of canned goods. The hotel keeper and the butcher each gave me a sled dog. I bought a .30-.06 Savage rifle and the hotel keeper let me have a ten-gauge shotgun for the winter. Later I bought a sled and a pair of snowshoes from the Indians. By this time, the winter freeze had set in, so I built a platform at the back of the log cabin on which I kept my fresh meat supply.

The next problem was dog feed. I was told that late in October and early in November there would be a run of coho salmon in the Chilkat River. When the fish arrived I got one of the Indians to show me how to catch them. Standing in the water near the bank he watched until he saw a salmon near the surface, often with his dorsal fin showing. He would then place his fourteen foot gaff about four feet above the fish and let the current take it over the fish. A firm yank would then impale the fish onto the gaff hook. With a little practice I was able in less than a week to catch 150 salmon. The fish froze almost at once and I was able to load them on the dog sled and take them to the cabin, where I stacked them on the platform with my meat supply.

During these preparations for the winter, I took time off to visit the village of Klukwan on foot and got in touch with individuals recommended by Father Kashaveroff. The informants were polite but not enthusiastic, and charged fifty cents an hour for their information. Then at the end of November, Frank Donley, a mixed blood who had been away for twenty years and had come to visit his mother's people in Klukwan, took up residence in an abandoned log cabin about two hundred yards from my cabin. He had first class marine engineer's papers and had served on destroyers during the First World War. Naturally we became good friends and he became an enthusiastic informant and an interpreter for some of the old people who could not speak English very well. He remembered much of the life in the village when he was a boy and often went to the village alone to gather information on questions that I had asked him. With Frank Donley's help the work proceeded well until April when I left for Sitka and Wrangel.

My stay near Klukwan was hard in that I had to do all the chores to maintain myself. By Christmas there were four feet of snow on the ground. I kept three paths free of snow, one to the wood pile, one to the water hole in the river ice, and one to the outhouse. The main road to Klukwan became packed hard by Indian and white dog sleds. Off these travel ways I had to go on snowshoes. This was my first field trip and although it was rugged I never felt better in my life. In the spring when the truck came by to take myself and my equipment to Haines I felt said to have to leave the old cabin.

The saddest part came when I had to leave the two dogs, Rusty and Skookum, in Haines. To me they were much more than work dogs. They were both of the same litter, a cross between a German shepherd and a malemute. They were companions. While I was waiting for the steamer at Haines, they insisted on sleeping next to my bed. I had already noted the deep attachment to sled dogs in Alaskan men. One had to be careful what one said about another man's dog, particularly his lead dog. Then one morning I boarded the steamer for Sitka.

In Sitka and later in Wrangell, life became easier. I lived in a hotel and walked to my informants' houses. The old men spoke English well. One had worked with John R. Swanton of the Smithsonian Institution and often spoke about him. In June I was back in Chicago.

In the fall of 1932 I met Malinowski quite by accident. He was giving a lecture at Northwestern University, which some of us at Chicago decided to attend. After the lecture Melville Herskovits invited Malinowski and us to a tea at his home. When Malinowski learned that I had just completed field research concerning the economy of the Tlingit, he explained that he was working on his book *Coral Gardens*, an account of Trobriand economics. He invited me to come to the London School of Economics the following year and offered to arrange a fellowship for me with the International African Institute. I, of course, agreed. The following month I received a letter from Malinowski informing me that all arrangements had been made.

During the school year of 1932–33 I took courses in anthropology and prepared my dissertation under the supervision of Professor A. R. Radcliffe-Brown. I passed my written examination for my Ph.D. degree in May 1933. That fall I left for England. After a year at the London School of Economics I left for Uganda, Africa, where I remained for two years. With another year in England it was not until the fall of 1937 that I returned to the United States to take my oral examination. The four years away from the United States explains the delay in getting my Ph.D.

After receiving my doctorate, I held short term teaching jobs at the University of Montana and the University of Missouri and an archaeological field job for the University of Texas. I joined the United States Government in 1939 and continued in government service for twenty-five years. Later I held two-year appointments at Cornell and the University of Southern California. I returned in 1967 to Corvallis, Oregon, where I did part time teaching until 1971 at Oregon State University. It is only now, at the urging of my colleagues, that my manuscript is being published.

In preparing the manuscript for publication, I have, as far as possible, modified the orthography, so that it will be more in keeping with modern usage, and have added to the Bibliography some important studies on the Tlingit that have been written since the time I did my field work. Except for a few minor corrections, the text remains essentially unchanged.

In my original thesis I acknowledged the kind assistance of the numerous individuals, many of them now deceased, who greatly aided my studies and my field work. These included professors Fay Cooper-Cole, A. R. Radcliffe-Brown, Robert Redfield, Leslie Spier, and Edward Sapir; student friends Drs. Opler, Hoijer, Eggan, and Sol Tax; and the innumerable Indian friends who supplied me with information, especially Frank Donley, my interpreter at Klukwan.

In addition to these, I wish to thank Dr. Thomas Hogg at Oregon State University, who helped me make arrangements for publication, and his colleague, Dr. John Dunn, who assisted in revising the orthography.

Kalervo Oberg
January 1973

Note on Orthography

The native terms were originally transcribed according to the orthography used by John R. Swanton in his work in Tlingit linguistics. These transcriptions have been revised in order to approximate a modern orthography and, hopefully, to avoid confusion in interpretation. The following changes have been made: [c] to [š], [x] to [x̣], [tł] to [ƛ], [dj] to [ǰ], [E] to [ʌ], [u] to [w] after x̣, k, q, g, and between vowels, ['] to [ʔ], and [·] to [ʔ] where it is clear that the geminate segment in rapid speech corresponds to a glottal stop or stricture in careful speech.

CONTENTS

ILLUSTRATIONS

THE SOCIAL ECONOMY
OF THE TLINGIT INDIANS

I

THE TLINGIT AND THEIR COUNTRY

Physical Environment

The country of the Tlingit Indians belongs to that magnificent bit of coast line which stretches from Puget Sound in the south to Glacier Bay and Yakutat in the north along the Northwest Coast of the North American continent. The mainland is formed by the high, rugged mass of the Coast Range, the mountains generally coming down to the water's edge, their summits capped with everlasting snows and their sides clothed with dense growths of spruce, fir, hemlock, pine, and cedar. The range is broken by many narrow inlets or fiords that wind their way far inland, often ending in glacier-fed, rushing mountain torrents.

The coast of the mainland is protected from the Pacific by a broad belt of islands and islets. Some of these, such as Vancouver Island, Queen Charlotte Islands, Prince of Wales Island, Baranof and Chichagof Islands, are of great size, Vancouver Island, the largest, being fifteen thousand square miles in area. The larger islands are also extremely mountainous and heavily forested; and all, both large and small, are connected by straits and passages, sounds and harbors, providing excellent means for navigation. Dangers, of course, exist in the strong tides and reefs which are present everywhere.

The northern end of this coast in southeastern Alaska is the home of the Tlingit. It stretches from latitude 54°40′ to about latitude 60° north and includes such islands as Prince of Wales, Kupreanof, Admiralty, Baranof, and Chichagof, besides numerous smaller ones. Portland Canal, Lynn Canal, Taku Inlet, and Glacier

Bay are the chief fiords. Into these inlets flow the rivers of this territory, forming passes into the interior. Huge glaciers flow down many of the valleys, breaking off bit by bit as they reach the salt water. These glaciers are, sad to relate, diminishing year by year. But the Tlingit tell of early times when the glaciers were much greater and when the waterways were choked with floating ice. Of these glaciers, Taku, Mendenhall, and Davis are the best known, but many mountain ravines still have their hanging glaciers, remnants of once mighty streams of ice.

As one proceeds northward into the Tlingit territory, the mountains become higher and steeper, more jagged and gray. The snow line comes down to about two thousand feet, the timber line to fifteen hundred. Above the timber, the gray granite ramparts break into rugged towers and slender serrated peaks and pinnacles; and every slope which is not too steep is covered by a mantle of snow. The cedar and fir disappear from the mainland coast, and the spruce and hemlock become more stunted. On the islands, the cedar holds its own, but is smaller in size than farther south.

The climate of this region is most variable. On the western coast of the islands, the full effect of the Japanese current is felt and the temperature is moderate. In summer, the average temperature of Sitka is about 60°F, in winter about 42°F. Rainfall ranges from sixty to eighty inches per year. As one nears the mainland coast, the temperature becomes more extreme, average summer temperature being about 70°F on the coast and 80°F or more in the valleys leading into the interior. Winter temperatures are extremely variable. At the mouth of an inlet, temperatures may vary about freezing point all winter, while twenty miles up the inlet there may be long periods of sub-zero weather. Rainfall, too, is heavy near the western slope of the coast range. Many places have over one hundred inches of rainfall a year. As the head of the inlets end in the mountain passes the snowfall is extremely heavy, a depth of twelve feet being quite common. In the whole region perfectly clear days are rare, even in the summer. During the six weeks which were spent in Juneau in July and August of 1931, only seven clear days were counted. When it is not raining, clouds and mists hide the surrounding country. But when the sun does come out, especially toward evening, the effect is magnificent and the rainy days are quickly forgotten.

Even the most rainy day in Alaska is not colorless. Perhaps it is the high latitudes, or the clouds, or the snow-capped peaks, or a combination of all—whatever the cause, there is a certain rhythmic change from mauves to gold and pinks which lasts the greater part of the day. Furthermore, it cannot be forgotten that this region, in summer, enjoys eighteen hours of sunlight out of twenty-four, and that one can watch the twilight change into dawn. In winter, of course, the days are correspondingly short, December and January often having less than six hours of sunlight a day.

History

The Tlingit came into contact with white people in the last quarter of the eighteenth century. Captain Cook was in Tlingit territory in 1789. English, American, French, and Russian traders visited the Tlingit until the Russians took control of the entire Tlingit country early in the nineteenth century. Baranov established a fort at Sitka about 1800, which was destroyed by the Tlingit several years later but was immediately rebuilt by the Russians.

In 1867, the United States bought Alaska from the Russians for $6,500,000, and established its military and legal machinery there. The Tlingit, however, were little affected by these changes. Their contact with the whites was through trader and missionary, and remained so until gold was discovered in the late 1870s. With the coming of mining camps, salmon canneries, and settlers, the contact became more intimate. Many of the Tlingit became wage laborers and left their villages, either temporarily or permanently. Along with this economic insecurity, owing to the dependence on wage labor, came whisky and syphilis. Once again, as in 1840 when smallpox killed thousands, the Tlingit were decimated by the white man's vices and diseases. These calamities, quite naturally, turned the Tlingit against the white men and there grew up a feeling of bitterness which was not found among the Indians on the Canadian side of the border. Missionaries did much to mitigate this feeling. As the young Tlingit learned to read and write and to adopt white men's ways, he found that he could get along fairly well.

During the present century, the Tlingit have become American citizens; they vote and pay taxes. This equality is really more apparent than real. The young Tlingit, who have been shown the better side of white culture by the missionary, again find themselves in economic and social competition with their more powerful neighbors. Favoritism and discrimination in the giving of fishing and trapping licenses, and the preference of white employers for white labor, make the lot of the Tlingit economically difficult. They find that they may be educationally and legally the equal of their white neighbor, but that in actual life they are discriminated against on account of their race.

Around most Alaskan towns, one now finds two types of Indian settlement: one, in which the old people live still endeavoring to maintain their old customs; the other, in which the educated Tlingit is trying to carve out his own destiny by fishing and following the old handicrafts, sending his children to the government Indian school, and depending as little as possible upon both the white people and the old folk in the other village.

Physical Type

In physical type, the Tlingit closely resemble their neighbors, the Haida and the Tsimshian. Boas (1895) gives the average height for men as 173 cm. They appear to be lightly built and, especially among the men, fat individuals are very rare. The cephalic index of 83.5 shows them to be distinctly brachycephalic. The face with an index of 77 gives an impression of great width and flatness. The nose with an index of 77.5 is low and broad, the bridge generally being concave. The lips are of a medium thickness and prognathism is not very pronounced. In color, the Tlingit are a slightly darker shade of yellow brown than the northern Chinese or Japanese. The hair is black, straight, and thick, graying only with great age. Baldness is rare and facial hair is very scanty.

The physical measurements compiled by Boas are average and give the impression of a homogeneous population. It is believed by many observers that there are two physical types present, not only among the Tlingit, but among all the Northwest Coast people; one, a round-headed, round-faced, flat-nosed type resembling the northern Mongoloid; the other, a medium-headed, long-faced type with a straight or slightly curved nose and high cheek bones.

The first type has less prognathism and is lighter in color than the latter. The first, also, has a fairly pronounced opicanthic eyefold which is not found in the latter. As one goes southward from the Tlingit, the longer-headed, long-faced type becomes more common. The first type is taller. Tables compiled by Boas (1895) show a gradual decrease in stature from Alaska south to the Fraser River. In the series for men, the stature decreases from 173 cm. among the Tlingit, to 169 cm. among the Tsimshian and Haida, to 164 cm. among the Kwakiutl and to 162 cm. among the coast Salish of the Fraser Delta.

Intermixture of the Aleut and other Eskimoid peoples of Alaska most probably has taken place, although the Tlingit firmly deny any such marriages. We know that the Russians used Aleut hunters almost exclusively along the entire coast of Alaska and British Columbia, and that these hunters became permanent residents in Tlingit country. Intermarriage with the Athapascan of the Yukon valley and the interior of British Columbia, and with the Haida and Tsimshian were, and still are, very common. Furthermore, slaves from among the Salish, Kwakiutl, and Nootka were freed and became residents in Tlingit villages.

Today, mixed bloods are very common, owing to early trader and miner contact. In Sitka Russian-Indian individuals are very numerous and of long standing, and one finds the nucleus of a new physical type among them. At present, marriages between Indians and whites are lessening in frequency, owing to the stabilization of the population. White settlers take up land or become settled fishermen, bring in their wives, and have little to do with the Indians.

Technology

Among the physical resources used by the Tlingit, fish are of primary importance. Five kinds of salmon are used: the large, fat, king salmon, which sometimes weighs as much as fifty pounds; the famous sockeye, which averages six or seven pounds; the coho or silver salmon, which averages ten pounds; the dog and the humpbacked salmon, which are much used but are considered of inferior quality as compared with the others. Of the deep sea fish, the cod, halibut, and herring are the most popular. The small, fat eulachon is used for making oil. Shellfish, such as the clam, oyster, sea urchin, and mussel are constant ingredients of the diet along with different kinds of algae and seaweed. Sea birds' eggs are also used whenever they can be obtained.

The country of the Tlingit is rich in wild animals and, even today, it is a hunter's paradise. The white-tailed deer, mountain goat, black bear, porcupine, marmot, and the snow-shoe rabbit are the commonest food animals. The tribes living on the mainland often take trips into the interior for brown bear, moose, bighorn sheep, and caribou. For their fur, the Tlingit hunt and trap the red, gray, and black fox, the wolf, the wolverine, otter, mink, beaver, marten, and lynx. Of the sea mammals, the fur and hair seal, the sea otter, and the sea lion are hunted for flesh and pelt. The whale is not hunted but dead carcasses are eagerly used for food whenever they drift ashore. Of the sea birds, the wild duck or mallard, the Canada goose, the pintail, the widgeon, and the teal are much used. The forest birds most commonly eaten are the blue grouse, willow grouse, spruce hen, and ptarmigan.

The spruce and hemlock are of great importance to the mainland people. The cottonwood, birch, jack pine, cypress, willow, alder, crabapple, and maple are also used. The yew tree is used for making of carved wooden dishes and bows. While the red cedar is the tree of primary importance on the Northwest Coast generally, it is of less importance among the Tlingit on account of its stunted size in that area.

Many species of berry bushes provide fruit for the Tlingit. Among the most useful are the high and low bush cranberry, the salmonberry, serviceberry, huckleberry, soapberry, wild currant, thimbleberry, and many species of swampberry.

Wild rice, wild celery, wild rhubarb, clover, many kinds of roots and tender stems are constantly used. The roots of the devil's club, the berry of the mountain ash and the powdered leaf of the skunk cabbage are used for medicinal purposes.

The essential tools of the Tlingit were the knife, chisel, wedge, adze, and hammer. The knife blade was made from shell, antler, or stone and was fastened to a wooden handle by being fitted into the wood and then lashed with sinew. The chisel was made of stone or antler and was used for carving wood. The wooden or stone wedges were sometimes quite large and were used chiefly for splitting off house planks. The adze, probably the most useful of tools, was made by fitting an antler or stone chisel to a wooden handle shaped like that of a flatiron. This hand adze was used for smoothing the wooden surfaces of planks and for making canoes. Adzes with long handles were also used for rough work. The hammer is actually a stone mallet or maul.

Native copper was used only for making the large copper shields which were used as potlatch goods. These shields were beaten out from raw copper found in the interior and brought to the Tlingit by the Athapascan traders.

Harpoons of many shapes and sizes, with points made of antler or bone, were used for fishing. The points were barbed either on one side or on both and fitted into a piece of yew wood with a sinew loop to which the cord was attached. This yew point-holder was then fitted into a six- or seven-foot cedar pole for throwing the harpoon at salmon in the river or at seals or porpoises in the sea. Fishhooks were made by lashing bone points and barbs on U-shaped pieces of wood. Weirs and traps of many kinds were made and used in the streams.

The spear was made by fastening a bone or shell point to a long handle and was used when hunting bears or mountain goats with dogs. The plain bow and arrow was in common use. The loop snare, pit, and deadfall were used for small game and birds.

Bending planks by scarring and seaming to make boxes with only a single seam or joint is quite common. This joint is carefully fitted and sewn together with spruce root or cedar withe. The bottom is sewn on in the same manner, making the box quite watertight. Wooden pegs are sometimes used for joining the wood. Watertight basketry is made from spruce root and cedar bark. Fish nets are made from strips of rawhide or sinew.

The Tlingit canoes are of two kinds, the small cottonwood dug-out used in the mainland rivers, and the large red cedar canoe made on the Prince of Wales Island by the Tlingit or obtained from the Haida through barter. The large cedar canoes are made from a single log, often being forty or fifty feet in length and able to carry as many as forty men. The stern and bow pieces are highly ornamented and are fitted on with spruce root thongs and wooden pegs. Fire is sometimes used in felling the tree but windfalls are always used when available. Fire is also used in aiding the hollowing-out process. The canoe is made wider by filling it with hot water and then having the gunwales pushed apart by stout cross-pieces. In the early days, the paddle and the pole were the sole means of propulsion. The sail was introduced by white men. With these canoes the Tlingit made voyages of hundreds of miles on their vast inland waterways.

The weapons of the Tlingit consisted of the bow and arrow, spears, long bone daggers, clubs made from the whale's rib, and a picklike weapon made from fastening a piece of pointed whale's rib to a handle. For fighting in canoes, paddles, with their points sharpened with bone, were used. The Tlingit also used armor made by lacing yew wood sticks, the thickness of one's finger, together to form a broad belt around the middle. Along with the armor, the warrior often wore a wooden helmet.

The Tlingit house is a low, square structure made from spruce or cedar planking. The frame consists of four corner-posts with four plates. In front, at each side of the doorway and at the back, a pair of taller posts support the two ridge poles. The frame is from thirty to fifty feet square, six feet high at the eaves and about fourteen feet high at the ridge. The walls are made by laying planks horizontally, the ends fitting into the grooved posts. Grooved planks placed from the ridge downwards form the roof, which has a smoke hole in the center. Inside, the posts, the plates, and the moldings over the doorway are richly carved with totemic crests. Near the back wall is a large screen almost reaching the roof with a large hole in the center. This screen is painted with totemic animals, birds, and spirits. Behind it are kept the ceremonial paraphernalia of the house-group, and through the hole in the center of the screen the chief of the house emerges on ceremonial occasions. The floor is of beaten earth, often being a foot or two below the doorstep. A central fire keeps the house warm. Sleeping platforms, covered with cedar bark mats, are arranged around the walls. The bedding is rolled up during the day and the platforms used for seats. From the roof beams hang platforms upon which are kept articles belonging to the inmates. Some houses have excavations in the floor near the fire for sweat-baths, others wall off a corner of the house for this purpose. There are no windows. The doorway and the smoke hole provide light and ventilation during the day and the fire serves as a lamp at night. A heavy mat covers the doorway.

Tlingit villages are uniformly built, consisting of a row of houses along a beach or along a river bank. Doorways always face the water. In front of the houses are racks for drying fish and houses for smoking them. Canoes are hauled up on the beach and protected from the sun by a covering of mats or bushes. Some distance behind the houses are the graveyards, one for each of the clans living in the village. Formerly, each clan had a funeral pyre on which the dead were cremated, their ashes being deposited in the totem poles standing before the houses. While the sanitary arrangements of the Tlingit are carefully secluded back in the bush behind the houses, the other refuse is thrown on the beach where dogs, gulls, and crows extract the last bit of nourishment from it.

At one time Tlingit villages were very numerous, dotting the mouths of all the important salmon streams. Even today, one can see where a village once stood by the large banks of clam shells and the absence of evergreen trees. Today, most of the villages are found near the white settlements. Originally, of course, trading posts were established near Indian villages and the tendency was for these villages to grow in size and to persist while the villages more distant from the white contact tended to disappear. Villages at the mouths of the larger rivers, such as the Stikine, Taku, and Chilcat, were formerly of great importance because they controlled the trade routes into the interior. The village at Wrangell at the mouth of the Stikine is still an important Tlingit settlement. From the old village of Taku at the mouth of the Taku River, the people have left for Juneau, the present capital of Alaska. Klukwan on the Chilcat River is the most primitive of the Tlingit villages. Sitka has been under white influence for over a century. Klawak, Kake, and Hoonah are important villages, each still containing several hundred people. The most northerly village is in Yakutat Bay and has less than a hundred inhabitants.

The Chilcat valley formerly supported about eight thousand [1] Indians living in four villages. Today, only two villages are inhabited with a combined population of less than a hundred. The people have either died off or have left to seek employment at the canneries or the mines. Other river valleys tell the same story —rows of empty houses or house sites. Sometimes a family may return to fish in the ancestral waters and live for a few brief weeks among the fast disappearing remnants of their past culture.

[1]. 1973 note: According to recent authorities, this figure appears exaggerated.

Outline of Culture

As the following chapters will deal specifically with the economic system of the Tlingit and its relation to their social structure and belief system, it will be necessary, at this point, to outline briefly the principal characteristics of Tlingit culture other than the technological basis already described. The culture of the Tlingit is a variation of the Northwest Coast type and is characterized by an economy based on fish, particularly the annual salmon run; settled villages; high development of woodwork; a social organization marked by lineages, clans, and phratries; and a ritual life centering around totemism, shamanism, secret societies, and the potlatch; and a form of art made famous by the totem pole.

Linguistically, the Tlingit are closely related to the Haida, both, in turn, being members of the great Athapascan language family. Unfortunately, the Tlingit language has not been exhaustively studied. What information we have comes from the works of Swanton (1908) and Boas (1917). The work of Boas has been used in making the following brief remarks on the phonetics and morphology of the language.

The most striking feature about the consonants is the absence of labials, the lack of almost all voiced fricatives, and the occurrence of very strong glottalized fricatives. The vowels have a well-marked high and low pitch of considerable range.

The denominative, predicative, connective, and formative elements of which the Tlingit sentence is built are monosyllabic almost entirely. From the simple nominal elements, new concepts are formed by composition. Verbal stems are never compounded to form complex verbal ideas.

These nominal and verbal stems are preceded by prefixes which serve to classify objects according to form. They undergo modifications according to the modal form of the verb and according to the definiteness of action in regard to object and time; while another modification designates generalized action or indefinite objects. Another group of modifications expresses definite time, and the correlated group, indefinite time. In verbal forms the classifiers are preceded by the pronominal subject which is closely associated with temporal and modal elements. Before these stands the pronominal object. Locative elements introduce the verbal complex. Certain modal forms are expressed by suffixes which follow the verbal complex.

Both nominal and verbal stems may be developed by means of suffixes which qualify the fundamental idea in regard to concepts of size, number, and time. The ideas thus expressed are diminutive, augmentive, number, certain types of repetition, and past tense.

In the pronominal forms, singular and plural are distinguished. Subjective, objective, and possessive pronouns are expressed by separate forms.

The modality of the sentence is expressed by a large number of adverbs; its relation to the other parts of the discourse is determined by conjunctions.

Grammatical processes are juxtaposition, prefixing, vocalic change, and loss of consonants. The position of word clusters and particles is comparatively free. There is no reduplication.

The art of the Tlingit is exemplified by all the material objects of his culture: his house, his canoes, his food boxes and dishes, and his tools and weapons. But it is in his ceremonial objects that the art reaches its characteristic expression. The carved house posts, screens, and plates, although parts of the house, serve religious ends, and may be treated as ceremonial objects. The totem poles, the hats, the masks, the Chilcat blankets, and the batons are objects of the highest artistic workmanship.

The art of the Tlingit, whether carving or painting, chanting or dancing, derives its themes from a rich and varied mythology. These myths account for man, for nature, and for the world of spirits, and are dominated by the adventures of the totemic spirits and the ancestors of the clan. Of these totemic spirits, the Raven is supreme. He is the culture hero who stole the sun and gave it to his people, stole the water and made the rivers of the Tlingit land, stole the fish where they were kept in a basket far out in the Pacific. But he was not always kind. He could be cunning, a cruel trickster, lustful, and gluttonous. He could never be depended upon and his trail was strewn with both good and evil deeds. Half of the Tlingit people claim to be intimately connected with the Raven spirit and call themselves the Raven phratry; the other half claim to be connected with the Wolf spirit and call themselves the Wolf phratry. Everyone must marry from the other phratry. Besides these two important totems there are many others who helped establish the numerous clans of the Tlingit. The ancestors of the clans met these beings in animal form and received supernatural power from them. In later days people met them in dreams and visions and made them the totem of their houses.

Besides the totemic legends there are stories of the adventures of the clan ancestors, their battles, hunts, contests of strength, and love affairs. There are stories of great shamans who fought one another with the aid of their spirit helpers. There are stories of feuds lasting for many years between clans, and stories of great potlatches given by clan chiefs. Most of these myths and legends, in turn, derive their form and color from the world of birds and animals. The raven is represented on the totem pole in one way, on the clan hat in another, and on the Chilcat blanket in still another. Individual artists add their own touches, but mythic figures can always be recognized by certain conventionalized marks: the raven by its long straight bill, the wolf by its long ears, the shark by its gill slits, the killer-whale by its dorsal fin with a hole in it, the bear by its paws, the beaver by its crosshatched tail, the frog by its belly, and the eagle by its curved beak. The medium of the artist forces him to use complex conventionalizations. The eagle painted on a food box, carved all the way around a hat, or carved on a round pole is difficult to recognize as the same object unless one is acquainted with the distinguishing mark of the totem. The outlines of the figure are clear, strong, and virile, showing economy and certainty on the part of the artist. The colors used are black and white, red and yellow, with blue and green as subsidiary colors. There is a certain strength and boldness in the color patterns of the Tlingit which become meaningful when one understands their mythology and social values.

The totem poles of the Tlingit are simple compared with those of the Tsimshian and Haida. Tlingit clans had fewer totemic crests than these clans and thus had fewer figures to represent. The original Tlingit totem pole was used for keeping the ashes of the dead. It was often a single figure mounted upon an undecorated pole. If the man belonged to the Raven phratry he used the raven figure in a form adopted by his clan; if to the Wolf phratry, he used the wolf figure. These were the primary phratry totems. Today, on the more complex poles, one finds either of these figures on top, depending upon the phratry to which it belongs, with the clan and house crests below. The poles at Wrangell are, perhaps, the best examples of Tlingit totem pole art. The poles at Sitka are Haida poles made by a Haida Indian by the order of one of the governors of Alaska. At Klukwan and Yakutat complex totem poles disappeared altogether and, in former days, were represented by the simple burial poles alone. This seems to indicate that the center of totem art development was around the mouths of the Nass and Sheena rivers in Tsimshian country and among the Haida on the Queen Charlotte Islands.

The house posts and screens of the Tlingit are far more important art forms than outside totem poles. The four corner posts are carved and painted, each telling the story of some clan ancestor. The screen is a plain surface painted with the totemic figures, the phratry emblem predominating.

The Chilcat blanket is considered by many as equal to the best weaving of the ancient Peruvians and Mexicans. The warp is made of a mixture of mountain goat's wool and cedar bark and is wound around two crossbeams. The woof is of mountain goat's wool and is woven in, three strands at a time, beginning from the top and working down. The patterns are woven in separately and represent the crest animals and birds in vivid colors of black, white, green, and yellow. The figures are broken up and the parts are arranged in the three sections of the blanket. Once the arrangement is understood, the totems can be easily seen. There are, of course, dots, bars, and borders which are purely decorative forms. The Chilcat blanket is a misnomer, for it is really a shawl-shaped robe which is worn on ceremonial occasions and is never used as a rug or blanket. The pattern of the Chilcat blanket came from the Tsimshian and was adopted by the Tlingit, the Chilcat people specializing in its production, owing to the ease with which mountain goat's wool could be procured in their district.

Of the ceremonial objects, the most important are the crest hats worn by the representatives of the important houses and clans. They are made of wood and shaped like a cone with the crest animal represented on top. Decorations of shell, weasel fur, and sea lion whiskers are placed around the crest figure.

Masks made of wood and painted to represent great animals and birds play a leading part in the dances. These masks are often controlled by the wearer by means of strings which blink the eyes, open the mouth, and protrude the tongue. Many masks are made so that the wearer can represent the changes of the mythical ancestor and totem from one form to another by opening the outer layer and showing another mask inside.

The ancient rattles were made in the form of birds, brightly colored or highly polished. The black oyster-catcher model was used by shamans only. The raven, eagle, and hawk models were used by the people. The rattle was made in two halves, several pebbles were put in, and the sides were then fastened together with sinew lacing. The batons were flat oblong pieces of wood fastened to a wooden handle and painted with the totemic emblems. Sometimes the hair of dead slaves would be fastened to the end of the batons.

The art of the Tlingit is intimately bound up with their religious life, which we can consider as consisting of totemism, shamanism, and magic. Totemism, as we have already seen, is made up of a series of beliefs about the nature and origin of man and the physical world. Its dogma is embodied in Tlingit mythology, and its ritual enters into all the important activities of their social life which will be treated later. Here, it is necessary to describe only the ritual of the chant and the dance, the elaborate exhibition of the clan totems, and the recitation of clan legends.

The dances take place within the house or, if the crowd is too large, outside. If they take place inside they are performed around the fire, the spectators sitting near the walls. In group dancing the themes differ but the impression, at least to the white observer, remains constant. The movements are rhythmic, keeping time to the two-four beat of the drum. The movements of the feet are the same throughout a single dance. The arm, body, leg, and shoulder movements vary and constitute the theme. The movements are powerful in that they require the entire strength of the body, which is held at an extreme tension giving the appearance of jerky movements. The dance progresses deliberately to completeness, leaving the observer with a feeling of balance and satisfaction.

The action is derived from the movements of animals. This is strikingly apparent in the head and shoulder movements, which resemble those of a deer stalking carefully, turning its head from side to side; or those of a bear or wolf as it is pursued—a few steps, a stop, and a turn to one side or the other. While the dance gives an impression of balance and harmony, there is about it a wildness that is of the sea and the forest, of the animals and the birds. The dancers seem to be on the borderland of demoniacal frenzy. My interpreter stated that the dances stirred him immensely, that they made him want to go hunting in the mountains or go on a war party. There is nothing in the dances to awaken sexual desire. The beauty of the human form is not considered. Words like power, energy, wildness, frenzy, most truly describe the spirit of Tlingit dances.

The chants accompanying the dances are conducive to fierce activity. The variation in time and range is slight. There is a theme but nothing that a white man would accept as a melody. Some chants have words, others repeat certain intonations. Here, again, animal sounds enter in—the howling of the wolf, the long, drawn-out blast of the deer, and the hooting of the owl are woven into the magical patterns. If one spends much time in the forests of the Northwest Coast, the chants of the Indians reveal themselves as conventionalized imitations of the animal sounds of that region. As in the dances, tenderness is lacking and a wild passion governs the presentation of the song.

The totemism of the Tlingit, of which we shall hear more later, is their group religion. There is a body of beliefs and a ritual to keep alive the social values which these beliefs represent. It is necessary for the working of his social order. The form and manner of telling the myths, the totemic crest objects, the songs and the dances constitute the art of the Tlingit. Shamanism among the Tlingit is a belief in spirits and in the power of man to invoke their aid. The totemic spirits come once, give power, and then remain separate, leaving the totemic crests as symbols of their power. The shaman's spirits, *yeiks,* on the other hand, must be invoked directly each time something is desired. There are a great number of these spirits who control weather, health, success in war, and other human undertakings. A successful shaman gets the aid of as many spirits as possible and, when he dies, endeavors to pass these spirits on to one of his nephews. At first, it would appear that the spirits are clan property but this view does not represent the true nature of the facts. It is true that many spirits are associated with certain clans and that they belong to certain regions but these spirits can be, and often are, used by shamans of other clans. There are spirits that belong to no clan and will aid anyone who can get in touch with them.

Enšukatanka is a spirit generally associated with the Kagwantan clan. It controls the weather and when one gets its help, one can make the weather bright or stormy at will. All shamans tried to get the aid of this spirit.

Šaxukintaxoni, also associated with the Kagwantan, foretells the future to the shaman. He lives in the mountains near Chilcat and has a special interest in these people. Chilcat shamans resent anyone else trying to use this spirit.

Ginauxoni lives in the Chilcat region and warns the shamans when enemies are coming.

Kuštaxa was once a shaman but changed into an evil spirit who takes the otter form. He robs the souls of people who are lost at sea or who die alone in the woods. He then changes the man's soul into another Kuštaxa spirit. Shamans having connections with this spirit are very much feared.

Yanaguxa is a messenger spirit that can be used by all shamans. He is sent to the weather or war spirit or anywhere the shaman wants him to go.

Tšakxo-yeik (eagle spirit) is associated with the Tluk'naxadi clan and is a war spirit.

Xustoxan-šauwe (sun woman) is also a Tluk'naxadi spirit and is used in healing the sick.

When an old shaman dies, those of his nephews who wish to become shamans sit around his body and try to get into a trance. The young man who remains in the trance the longest and satisfies the elders of the house becomes a novice. He is then made to fast and keep away from women. After a week or so he goes into the forest accompanied by eight of his kinsmen. They eat only dried salmon once a day and bathe in a stream. Something supernatural is expected to happen and everyone is looking for a sign. The best sign is when a bird or animal is seen to drop dead. This tells the novice that he is in touch with a certain spirit. There are signs for each spirit. When the bear, otter, mink, or eagle falls dead, the novice cuts out its tongue, splits it, and wraps it in a little bundle of hemlock bark, grass, and devil's club. This is his medicine, *kutš*. Whenever a shaman bathes, he rubs his body with his *kutš*, and he uses it in all his performances.

A group of shamans often live in caves for long periods of time perfecting their powers. When living in the village they usually have houses of their own and a shrine in the woods near by, for if a woman, during menstruation, were to see a shaman's *kutš* it would lose its power. When a young man has proved that he possesses his uncle's spirits, he inherits his paraphernalia, consisting of charms, rattles, pointing bone, masks, drum, songs, and dances. When a shaman dies, his body is put in a little hut on a hill away from the village. If he has no successor, his property is buried with him. The Tlingit live in great fear of shaman's graves, and on no account will they disturb one.

Shamans cure the sick by spiritual aid. When a performance is to be held, women who are menstruating are requested to leave the house. The shaman then sits at the head of the patient and begins to drum and chant. He will finally state whether the patient will recover or die. Sometimes he will draw out objects from the body which have caused the illness. He may also feel the body until he finds the foreign object that is causing the trouble, and then he will ask a spirit to take it away. The Tlingit claim that in the old days the shamans never used medicine, herbs, or magic, but always spirits. Today, shamans use spirits, pagan and Christian, patent medicines, and all types of spells and amulets.

Witch hunting, in the old days, was a favorite occupation of the shamans. If anyone fell ill, witchcraft was suspected, and the sick person's relatives would hire a shaman to try to discover the evildoer. The shaman would go into a trance beside the sick man after prolonged drum beating and chanting. Whoever the shaman mentioned as the witch or sorcerer was instantly killed.

War offered the greatest scope for the shaman's powers and no Tlingit war party ever set off without its shaman. Before the party left, the shaman went into the forest in search of signs, conducted the training of warriors, and saw to it that all the rules were kept by the women while the men were on the warpath. Often a battle was conducted entirely by shamans who pitted the spirits of their side against those of the other. When in the enemy's territory, the shaman lay in the bottom of the canoe, covered with mats, and directed the movements of the warriors.

When the war parties were in actual contact, each side shouted what their spirits would do. "A shower will put out your fires tonight," one party would call. "A sand spit will appear in the bay before you," the others replied. This was kept up until one side believed that the spirits of the other were stronger. This might even decide the dispute, and the attackers would withdraw to their home.

The shamans among the Tlingit, at one time, were very important, much more so than among the other Northwest Coast peoples. They were wealthy and influential, and often competed with one another in performing miracles. When performing, they wore masks representing their spirits and sang songs telling of their power and of the deeds they had performed in the past. Among the Tlingit, the shamans and their spirits were considered in a different category from the totemic spirits. They feared these shaman spirits which could be used by individuals to work harm upon other individuals. Totemism was social and integrative while shamanism was individual and disintegrative.

Magic, among the Tlingit, was an individual matter. There were no collective magical rituals before hunting or fishing. Individuals would try to improve their luck by incantations and the use of amulets, by observing food taboos and sex continence. Amulets were made of bits of grass, feathers, and animal hair, and they were passed on from a man to his sister's son. Rights to use these amulets could be given away but the original owners could still keep on using them. Friends often exchanged their good luck amulets. These objects were fastened to spears and, later, to guns. Every canoe possessed one.

Harmful objects also existed which, if brought into contact with tools and weapons, would make them ineffective. Tlingits still point to guns which they cannot use because magic has been practiced over them. Whenever a party sets out on a long voyage, the people are careful to wash out the canoe, to see that no magic bundles have been hidden in it, and to install their own best amulets.

When felling a tree for canoe building, a man may speak to the tree, "I shall cut you down, tree. You will not twist and warp, tree. You will not have knot holes, tree." He will carefully burn the bark and branches that have been left after the canoe has been made. A man also talks to wild animals and sea mammals when he is hunting them. At no time may a person talk in derogatory terms about animals for fear of insulting them. The Tlingit, it was observed, will work for hours making a hole in the frozen earth to bury the carcass of a fur-bearing animal after the pelt has been removed. They believe that if the body is not correctly treated, the spirit of the animal will be displeased and will warn all the other animals.

Witchcraft or black magic was practiced to harm one's enemies or rivals. To make a person ill, a bit of powdered human bone was put in his food. By getting possession of an enemy's clothing, hair, or excrement, one could work harm on him. Evil magic existed in human corpses, and if anyone was seen wandering around a shaman's grave at night he might be suspected of witchcraft. Magic played an important part in Tlingit life, but belief in spiritual powers was greater. The Tlingit always was on the lookout for signs in the flight of birds, the cry of animals, the bending of branches on the forest trail, the color and formation of clouds, and his own dreams. These signs revealed to him what the spirits intended and he would govern his actions accordingly. Sexual continence was observed before all important undertakings for weeks and months at a time. While the men were out on a war party, the women had to sit as if they were in a war canoe and go through the movements of their husbands. Fasting and bathing in the sea were generally observed before all important undertakings by both men and women.

In the old days, when a Tlingit woman was about to give birth, her husband and his brothers would build a small hut for her at the back of the house. Here the woman would stay for a week or two before the birth was due. Her sisters-in-law would attend to her, bringing her food, and massaging her abdomen to make the birth easier. An experienced masseuse claimed to know whether the child was a boy or a girl and whether twins were due.

Only women attended births but in difficult cases a shaman was asked to help. The old way of giving birth was to dig a shallow pit, line it with moss, and drive a wooden stake in the center; the prospective mother would squat in this pit, hold on to the wooden stake, and give birth to the child. The women attending her would stand around chanting, and when the child was born they would cut the umbilical cord with two stone arrow points and fasten the loose end to the woman's big toe until she had freed herself of the placenta. The child was wiped dry with fine clean moss, wrapped in cedar bark, and given to the mother.

After a day or two the mother would walk back into the big house and the little birth hut would be destroyed.

At puberty, girls were put behind a screen for as long as four months to one year. The higher the rank of a girl the longer she remained in seclusion. During this time her mother taught her songs, legends, manners, and the duties of a woman. No man was permitted to see her and she was not permitted to look at the sea, tools, weapons, or ceremonial articles for fear that she would bring misfortune to the house. When the girl came out of seclusion she was ready for marriage and her father and mother guarded her chastity, for it was highly valued in a bride.

At the age of six or seven, the boys went to stay permanently in their mother's brother's house, where they were educated and trained in the duties of life. The details of this training are discussed later.

Cross cousin marriage among the Tlingit was the rule. When a young man decided to marry he had to get the permission of his uncle and the girl's parents. His uncle or his mother's sister acted as go-between. The uncle helped the boy to amass the bride gift necessary to validate a marriage. The bride gift is returned only if the bride died soon after marriage without leaving a marriageable sister or if she turned out to be a poor wife.

Burial was by cremation. The body was washed, dressed, and seated at the head of the house and around it the people feasted for four days. At night the women wailed over the body. Food was put into the fire so that the spirits of the dead ancestors could eat. On the fourth day, the body was placed on a large pile of logs and burned. The ashes were then placed in a small box until a totem pole could be erected, at which time they were placed inside it.

II

SOCIAL ORGANIZATION

Every Tlingit is born into one of three matrilineal totemic phratries in Tlingit society. He is either a Tlaienedi, a Šinkukedi, or a Neχadi. If he is a Tlaienedi, he calls himself a Raven; if he is a Šinkukedi, he calls himself a Wolf; and if a Neχadi, an Eagle. The Neχadi, however, are so few in number that they may be neglected here, and we may speak of the Tlingit as Ravens and Wolves, each person referring to a member of the other phratry as his "opposite." The members of a phratry consider themselves blood relatives and prohibit marriage within the group.

What is more important to a Tlingit is the fact that he is born a member of a clan. The clan has a name denoting its place of origin, a story of its genesis, and a history of its migration. Like the phratry, the clans are exogamic, matrilineal, and totemic. But, while the phratry is the ceremonial unit, the clan is pre-eminently the political unit.

A Tlingit also finds himself a member of a specific house-group. It is in this group that he is educated, carries on his important economic activities, and meets the important crises of his life.

Finally, there is the family, which, among the Tlingit, consists of a man, his wife or wives, and their children. Economically and politically the family is of minor importance. It is in the matter of rank that it always plays its part. Owing to the avunculate and the fact that the father and the children are members of different phratries, the family has little unity.

Hence, in a Tlingit village there are always members of at least two phratries. Furthermore, in a village there are local divisions of two or more clans. Each local division of a clan, in turn, is made up of a number of house-groups, and each house-group has a number of families. The village is a loose organization of clans, often bitterly contesting.

Before describing the form and function of each of these social groups in detail, it is necessary to explain the different kinds of relationships which exist between individuals, for it is out of these personal relationships that the groups themselves are formed. This takes us, then, to the kinship system of the Tlingit Indians. This system has twenty-two kinship terms which I shall endeavor to explain. It must not be forgotten, however, that there are a great number of descriptive terms which I have no space to treat here other than to point out the most important situations in which they occur (Swanton 1928; Durlach 1928).

Taking ego's generation as zero, we may speak of the parents' generation as the first ascending and the grandparents' as the second ascending generation. In the same way, we may speak of ego's children's generation as the first descending and the grandchildren's as the second descending generation.

In the second ascending generation there is but one term, *lilk'ʷ*, which is applied to one's mother's and father's parents and all their phratral brothers and sisters. The ego's relationship to any member of this class is one of deepest respect. He must always permit a *lilk'ʷ* to speak first and he must always address his *lilk'ʷ* by the relationship term. Grandparents do not form active members of the society and are thus removed from the opposition groups. They form a repository and final authority for myths and rituals.

There are six kinship terms in the first ascending or parents' generation. First of all, there are the terms for father, *iš*, and mother, *ẋa*. The relationship between mother and child is that which we find among most people. Even after a boy leaves his parents' house and goes to stay with his mother's brother, the mother still keeps in close contact with him and is important in the final selection of his mate. Theoretically, at least, the father has little to say about the upbringing of his son. The belief is that he is too soft-hearted and will not put his son through the necessary training. But the important fact to remember is that a son is not of his father's clan and phratry. The son belongs to the clan and phratry of his mother and, therefore, the father is not qualified to train a child in the customs and lore of a group which is socially opposed to him. The father, of course, is compensated by being allowed to bring up his sister's son. Actually, however, the tie between father and son is strong and, in many instances, a son returns to his father's village and there he builds a new home.

Daughters, on the other hand, always remain with their father and mother until they are given in marriage. A daughter, also, is put through careful training in domestic activities and in social and ceremonial deportment. The higher the rank of a girl, however, the less work she will be required to do but the more important will be her ceremonial duties. At puberty, a girl, in the past, went through a period of seclusion, after which she was carefully guarded by her parents until she was taken in marriage by a man of equal or of greater rank.

The mother's eldest brother, *kak*, is a man of great importance in Tlingit society, for upon him falls the burden of educating the coming generation of males. Economically, ceremonially, and politically, the interests of the maternal uncle and the nephew are the same. At the death of his uncle the young man takes over his uncle's property, position, and intrigues of the house.

The mother's sister, *λakʼʷ*, is also of great importance. Literally, the term *λakʼʷ* means "little mother" and, in fact, that is her position. A man treats his mother's sister with the same respect as his mother. She, in turn, takes his part in quarrels and is ever ready to give him advice. She also acts in the selection of a mate for him and she acts as a messenger between the parents of the girl and the boy.

Of much less importance is the father's brother, *sani*. A young man treats his *sani* with all the respect due to an older person in the opposite phratry. But if the *sani* becomes his stepfather then the relationship is much like that between father and son. A girl, on the other hand, may marry her father's brother, although this type of marriage is rare.

The father's sister, *at*, is a person of importance, because marriage with her is considered the most desirable match. The relationship here is free and easy, befitting that between men and women who are potential mates.

The mother's brother's wife, although important in the life of every young man, is distinguished by a descriptive term only. This is also true of the mother's sister's husband, of the father's sister's husband, and the father's brother's wife.

In speaking of individuals of one's own generation, a person uses five denotive terms. A man calls his older brother *hunx* and his younger brother *kik'*. Among the Tlingit, age is of great importance and it can easily be seen why a man distinguishes between his older and younger brother, for every older brother has precedence over his younger brother in inheritance, authority, and ceremonial activities. A man distinguishes his sister by the term *ẋak*.

A woman applies the term *šatx* to her older sister and the term *kik'* to her younger sister. The difference in their respective social positions accounts for this, exactly as in the case of the brothers. A woman distinguishes her brother by the term *ik*.

The relationship between brothers is the closest, for they are not only clansmen, but live in the same house and carry on many activities together. A sister, on the other hand, must avoid her brother's presence and never come into contact with him. When he comes into a room she must leave but, at the same time, she must attend to his wants and see that he is well cared for if he happens to be staying at her home. Under special circumstances in which a brother is very young and the family happens to be disorganized, a sister may care for her brother until he grows up.

In the Tlingit relationship system, there are no denotive terms for either parallel or cross-cousin. Mother's sister's children are classed with one's own brothers and sisters. Mother's sister's sons who are brought up in the same house as ego act together with ego as brothers. The terms for younger and older siblings apply as well to one's mother's sister's children. Father's brother's children are not considered relatives unless their mother happens to be related to one's own mother. In any case they are distinguished by a descriptive term.

One likewise applies descriptive terms to father's sister's son and daughter. Father's sister's daughter, whom one generally marries, is usually called *at*, the term applied to her mother. In the same manner, her brothers are called *sani*, the term applied to father's brother. Mother's brother's children are also descriptively designated. But they, likewise, fall into the *sani* and *at* group, being members of the opposite phratry.

In the first descending generation there are four kinship terms. The first two are *yit* for son and *si* for daughter. It must be noted that when a woman uses these terms they apply to members of her own phratry and clan and, as has already been observed, there is a close bond between them. In the case of the husband, however, *yit* and *si* apply to members of his opposite phratry and the bond is not nearly as close as that between mother and child.

The term *kelk'* is applied to one's sister's children by a man and this, of course, implies the uncle-nephew relationship. The term *kalk'ʷ* is applied to one's brother's children by a woman. It follows, from what has already been said, that a woman calls her sister's children *yit* and *si*—son and daughter—and that a man also designates his brother's children by these terms. The mates of the above-mentioned relatives are descriptively designated.

In the second descending generation there is but one term, that for grandchildren, *tšxank'*. As in the case of grandparents, grandchildren do not participate in the larger social activities of ego's generation and are thus treated as a single class. Yet it cannot be forgotten that a man's sister's daughter's sons come to live in his house, that he gives them names, and treats them as honorable descendants.

Finally, we must say something about the terms denoting relationship by affinity. Of these there are only five. *Xox* is used by a woman for her husband and *sat* by a man for his wife. In-laws of the same sex and generation as the speaker are termed *kani*. Brothers-in-law form close friendships, and it is through his brothers-in-law that a man makes his desires and grievances known to his opposites. The term *wu* is used for father-in-law, and the term *tšan* for mother-in-law is generally used. There exists a strict mother-in-law avoidance among the Tlingit. A man must never address his mother-in-law, nor she him. A woman must always try to get away from the presence of her son-in-law. She bows her head if she must pass him. All conversation is carried on through an intermediary. These restrictions, however, do not extend to the daughter-in-law, though, naturally, she must always retain a respectful attitude toward both her parents-in-law. She never addresses them until they address her; then she may reply. There are no further restrictions on her conduct. The same rules apply in the case of a young man and his father-in-law.

The above forms a brief description of the denotive relationship terms and some of their functions. It will still be necessary to mention the extent of some of these terms. The term * liłk'ʷ* is applied to one's grandparents and to members of their generation irrespective of phratry. The same is true of the term *tŝxank'*, the grandchild denotive, which also cuts across sex and phratry.

The term *λak'*, sister, is applied by a man to all women of his own phratry and generation. The term *hunx*, older brother, and *kik'*, younger brother, are used by a man to denote the older and younger men of his own generation and phratry, respectively. Likewise, a woman applies the term *šatx* to all older women of her phratry and generation and the term *kik'* to the younger women. She applies the term *ik* to all men of her phratry and generation.

The term *yit*, son, is used for one's own son and all the boys of his phratry and generation. The same is true for the term *si*, daughter. A man applies the term *kelk'* to his sister's children and to all members of their phratry and generation. A woman applies the term *kalk'ʷ* to her brother's children and to all the children of their phratry and generation.

Because of the sororate, the term *xox*, husband, is applied by an unmarried woman to her sister's husband. Reciprocally, a man calls his wife's unmarried sister by the term *sat*, wife.

On the whole, the Tlingit are averse to using relationship terms. This is less true of minors, women, and the aged, but men of middle age avoid these terms in favor of names and nicknames. The reason for this is the Tlingit's inordinate concern for matters of rank, rivalry, and pride. It was often dangerous to use relationship terms unless one were positively certain of their correct application, particularly when the two people speaking were of approximately equal age. Ceremonially, however, a man uses these terms constantly. Speaking to his own clan, during a ceremonial a young man would say, "my uncles and younger brothers." If he were older than the majority of his clansmen, he would say, "my younger brothers and nephews." In addressing his opposites, he would use the terms, "father's brothers," "father's sisters," or just "fathers," or "grandfathers." A member of a more remote clan could be addressed by "brother-in-law." The term "son" would be used on special occasions. The term "our grandfathers of old" emphasizes the connection of the clans and is used on the most special occasions.

The House-Group

So far we have analyzed, in a brief way, the fundamental kinship terms of Tlingit society and have emphasized the attitude which these terms of relationship imply. We shall now observe how these relationships are arranged in the structure of the house-group, how they are related to the clan and phratry, and how they formalize the behavior of the individuals composing these groups. It can be said that the house-group is the most important unit of economic and political security and, as such, participates in the larger ceremonial activities of the village and tribe.

Inasmuch as this paper is a study of the economic aspect of Tlingit society, many of the economic functions of the house-group will be left for further treatment, and attention here will be focused on such aspects as ownership, inheritance, marriage, rank, generation, descent, education, and ritual.

First of all, then, let us examine the composition of the house-group. To put the matter as briefly as possible, the male membership of a house-group is made up of (1) a number of brothers of ego, including his mother's sister's sons, (2) the sons of the sisters of these men, (3) the sons of the daughters of these sisters. In other words, there are generally three or more generations of males in each house-group who are related as members of a lineage through women in the associated house-group. In any two generations, men are to one another as mother's brother to sister's son. The grown men have wives, who may or may not come from a different house-group but who are always of a different clan and phratry. There are, of course, the children; but, as has already been pointed out, the boys leave their father and mother between the age of six and seven and go to live in the house of their mother's brother, the daughters remaining in the house of their parents until marriage when they, too, leave and go to live in the houses of their respective husbands. However, if a girl marries her father's sister's son, she will remain in the house of her father and mother.

Thus, we see in the house-group a close body of male kin of the same lineage, clan, and phratry. The bonds holding these individuals together are of the strongest possible nature. Let us take, first of all, brothers. The terms younger brother and older brother are applied to the respective men of one's own generation. There is a fundamental principle of social identity and equality defining the relationship of brothers. This comes out in the basic factors in life, as ownership, enterprise, inheritance, and leadership. The house, important ceremonial objects, slaves, large canoes, important arms—such as guns—trade goods, and many of the utensils are the common property of the house-group. The important food gathering activities of salmon fishing, oil making, berry picking, hunting, and trading are carried on jointly by members of the house-group. In the house the consumption of food is in common. It is prepared around a central fire and often ladled out of the same cooking box. Tools, weapons, clothing in use, and products of one's own enterprise are individually owned, providing the group as a whole has no need of these objects. In matters of ownership and enterprise, the principle is the house-group first and the individual second.

Just as the house-group as a whole, and brothers in particular, stand together economically, so in matters of feud or of minor dispute they form a solid front against all external infringements. Ceremonially, they act as the primary unit. Feasts, potlatches, and raids were often initiated by house-groups. These economic, political, and ceremonial obligations of one member of a house-group to a member of another house-group are here treated as social obligations and are in no way connected with individual sympathies and sentiments. Such psychological forces, of course, enter in to complicate the matter, just as often weakening house-group solidarity as strengthening it.

The oldest male is generally the house chief, or, as the Tlingit denote him, *yitsati* ("keeper of the house"). The *yitsati* does not own the house nor the ceremonial articles but holds them in trust for the others. He is not a war leader nor does he lead economic activities. This does not imply that he has nothing to say in these matters; if he is an able individual his words will carry weight. The *yitsati* is pre-eminently a ceremonial leader, a repository of myth and social usage, and an educator of the young of the house-group. The *yitsati* does not take part in common labor. He does, however, carry on the trading activities of the house-group and, of course, takes part in ceremonial labor, such as house building and burial.

He sleeps behind the screen at the back of the house where the sacred articles of the house-group are kept. On ceremonial occasions he comes out through the round opening in the center of the screen and addresses the house-group or initiates a ceremonial performance. When important visitors arrive they are led into the house by the younger men, and the *yitsati* greets them by vacating his seat directly before the ceremonial opening in the screen and offering it to the most important guest.

The *yitsati* also represents the house in the clan councils. Outside of the ceremonial and ritual occasions when the *yitsati* becomes a symbol of house-group unity, he takes his place around the fire with his kinsmen, the women, and, in former days, the slaves. The younger men, if they have been hunting individually, are obliged to bring choice bits of meat as gifts to the *yitsati*.

Between the *yitsati* and his brothers there is no sharp division. They are all considered of equal social rank. Age, however, forms a natural sequence and rhythm in the social relationship between brothers. Priority in leadership, ceremonials, and inheritance is always given to the oldest brother. When a *yitsati* dies his place is taken by a brother next to him in age. With this position go all the prerogatives attached to it. There is no distinction made between blood brothers and classificatory brothers, age being the determining factor. Only when a man is obviously incapable of filling the position is he passed over and a brother next to him selected. Thus, it is possible for every male member of the house-group to hold the office of the *yitsati*.

The relationship between the mother's brother and sister's son or, more generally, between uncles and nephews, is, likewise, complex and strong, but of a different kind from that of the relationship between brothers. As we have seen, there is a fundamental equivalence between brothers, the oldest always being the social representative of all the others, but not the overlord and ruler. Between uncles and nephews, on the other hand, there is the basic differentiation of generation with all the social significance which that implies. The differentiation is based on authority. The mother's brother has the same general authority over his sister's sons which fathers in some patrilineal societies have over their own children. As has already been mentioned, the *yitsati* has the duty of training the young men. But the respect of the nephews for the *yitsati* is also shown to the other uncles of the house-group.

As soon as a sister's son comes to stay with his mother's brother, he is put through a rigorous physical and mental training. The older Tlingit men still look back with pride at the cold baths they had to take when they were boys. The uncle would take the boys to the seashore or to the river bank and force them to plunge into the cold water. If the river was frozen then a hole had to be made in the ice to allow for the morning plunge. Once the boys were out of the water the uncle switched their bodies with boughs until their skins became red. He would then force them to run up and down on the beach. After the bath the boys had food and then the uncle spoke to them about manners, customs, and the history of the clan. During the rest of the day the boys watched the domestic activities of the older men. Special evenings were set aside for the telling of myths, and for the explanation of the sacred clan emblems. Officially, boys did not take an important part in the economic activities until after puberty. They did, however, perform services at feasts and potlatches, acting as ushers and messengers, and passing gifts from their uncles to their visitors.

While the boys were still young, their aptitudes and desires became evident, and, as there were specialists, like hunters, shamans, and carvers in the house, the boys began to cluster about the various uncles who pleased them and whom they wished to follow. The *yitsati* would present the oldest nephew to visitors, who often came from other Tlingit villages. The oldest nephew would thus get to know the important clans and the leading people of his society.

The nephews were, therefore, constantly under the strict authority of their uncles, and could do little without their consent. They also, on the other hand, had a definite set of rights to the house-group and to Tlingit society generally which came to them through their uncles. They had a right to the best kind of economic security that their society could offer, and they took the social positions vacated by their uncles. Within the house-group a nephew had the right to use his uncle's tools and weapons without asking his uncle's permission, although he was expected to do so. After property, privileges, honors, and wives passed from one uncle to another, they finally came to the oldest nephew. Thus we see that while the relationship of uncle and nephew was one of superordination and subordination, of authority and obedience, the bonds between them included every conceivable economic, legal, ritual, and marital relationship. Their relationships were equally strong and equally numerous looked at from either end, that of the uncle or that of the nephew. The complementary nature of this relationship contrasts well with that existing between a master and his slave which is also one of authority and obedience, but in which the rights are all one way. The slave had no legal right, even to his own life.

Daughters, as has been mentioned, remained with their parents until marriage. Like the boys, they, too, got a thorough training in clan regulations and customs. Girls of the nobility did very little work. In the houses of wealthy chiefs, every girl had a slave woman who saw to her wants. As slave labor became more important in Tlingit society, women became less important from an economic standpoint, and their functions became ceremonial. At puberty every girl went through a period of seclusion, ranging from four months to one year. As a rule, the longer a girl remained in seclusion, the higher people considered her rank. During this period, the girl observed certain food taboos, and was not allowed to look at men, or the sea, or hunting and fishing gear. While in seclusion she was instructed in the ways of the clan, its importance and history, so that she would know her rank and duties when once she was married. The function of the girl's puberty rite was to initiate the girl into society. There was a fundamental change in her relations to the people around her after she had gone through this ritual. Girls and boys, before puberty, were permitted the greatest familiarity with one another. There was no effort on the part of the elders to prevent the natural sex relations that developed in the growing children. But after puberty all this was changed. The initiated girl was not permitted to have any sexual relations, for her chastity was highly regarded by everyone. Parents made their daughter sleep on a shelf above their own bed to make sure that she was not molested. After puberty the relationship between brother and sister became one of strict avoidance. At the termination of the girl's puberty rite she was publicly presented at a great feast and potlatch given by her house. And, as was natural, young men were able to make judgments about girls and to make their wishes known after the ceremony. Thus, a girl's parents were careful to train her well and to guard her chastity after the puberty rites in order to secure a large bride price and to get a son-in-law of high rank.

Besides the above mentioned relatives and their wives and children, there was, formerly, a number of slaves in the more wealthy houses. These slaves were generally purchased from tribes further to the south of the Tlingit, for the Tlingit rarely took part in the slave raids. Although the slaves were used for carrying on the menial tasks of gathering wood and fetching water and for paddling canoes, they were primarily used for ceremonial purposes. At great potlatches where the important crests of the clans were displayed, slaves were killed or freed in great numbers to give these crests value. When slaves were freed they were permitted to go wherever they wished, but, as many of them had been slaves in a house for years, they had lost all hope of returning to their own house and so they sometimes remained in the house as members. Many of them married Tlingit mates of the lower class, their children thus becoming incorporated into one or the other of the clans and house-groups. Even today one meets individuals among the Tlingit who are ostracized by the best people because of slave blood. Freed slaves often became people of considerable importance, especially as carvers, dancers, or sorcerers. The Chilcats still speak of a certain freed slave who became one of the greatest ceremonial performers.

So much for the composition of the house-group and the chief types of social relationships existing within it. We shall now analyze the relationship between the various house-groups, in order to see how they modify the behavior of the individual, and to see what character they give to the village and tribe. The primary contact which one house-group has with another is through marriage. It is through marriage that new members are incorporated into this group. Women often come into the house as wives and permanent members. Sister's sons come in as permanent members. Therefore, as marriage is the determining factor of the house-group and of its linkages to the society at large, its importance can scarcely be overemphasized. We shall, therefore, take up the various types of relationships in marriage and show their effects upon the house-group.

There are four kinds of relatives that a man may marry, namely, father's sister, brother's daughter, father's sister's daughter, and mother's brother's daughter. The ideal form of marriage is that with one's father's sister. Through this kind of marriage, the nephew who succeeds his uncle is also his grandson. The

Tlingit deem it highly desirable for two reasons: (1) because it makes the successor to the *yitsati* his closest possible relative, being at once his sister's son and his son's son, and (2) because the status of the successor is more certain to be equal to that of his predecessor. As a complement to this there is marriage with a brother's daughter. This kind of marriage brings on immediate successors to the house-group as the boys soon leave for the house of their mother's brother. These two types of marriage are, however, not common for they imply marriage outside of one's own generation. For one thing a father's sister or a father's brother is an individual of considerably greater age than a father's son or daughter and, therefore, there is a natural aversion to that type of marriage. Second, the father's sister or brother is probably already married which cuts down the likelihood of this type of marriage.

The commonest type of marriage and that which the young men also prefer is that with one's father's sister's daughter. This kind of marriage correlates with the fourth type, namely, that with one's mother's brother's daughter. In fact, the fundamental marriage pattern is one with a woman who is at once the father's sister's daughter and the mother's brother's daughter, for the father's sister is often married to one's mother's brother.

The principal factor involved in these marriage regulations is rank—the social rule demands that one always should marry his or her equal. The rank of an individual is always taken from one's father and mother and is usually reflected in the amount of the bride price. But while social usage demands equality, individual forces often disrupt this equilibrium, for everyone, as a rule, wishes to marry a mate of as high a rank as possible.

Another factor of great importance to the Tlingit is material wealth. The potlatch motive is the center of their social life. Hence, every precaution is taken to keep property within the group. The house and ceremonial objects, such as crests and coppers, do not leave the house-group, but pass from uncle to nephew. There is, however, a great amount of individual wealth in the form of hides and pelts which the men of the house-group accumulate for themselves by their own efforts. The fixed wealth in crests and coppers, of course, comes out of this fluid wealth so that its importance cannot be exaggerated. Now the rule for the inheritance for this individual property is that it goes to the wife of the dead man who is at liberty to dispose of it as she pleases. It follows naturally that if she remarries she takes it with her, but if she remains unmarried she distributes it among her own brothers.

Another form of property transfer is the payment for ceremonial labor. During house building and burials this expenditure is considerable.

We have already mentioned that matters of kinship, rank, and property are of the utmost importance to the Tlingit. We shall now see how Tlingit society has developed means for the protection of these rights. Marriage, as we have seen, is the tie which binds houses together, which affects matters of rank and prop-

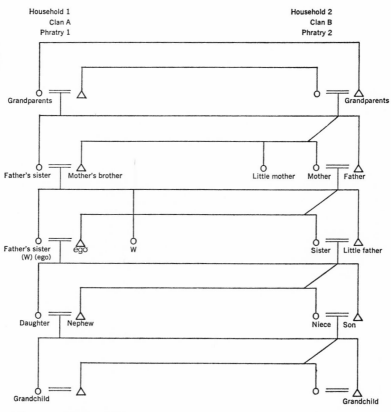

Figure 1. Basic marriage pattern. Terms remain the same for female ego

erty. Therefore, we shall see how the marriage rules of the Tlingit specifically correlate with these factors.

Marriage with a father's sister or a brother's daughter is, because of age, rather unusual, so that we have left marriages with a father's sister's daughter or a mother's brother's daughter. As we have already pointed out, the Tlingit desires a man of the closest kinship connection as his successor if rank can possibly permit this. Thus marriage with a father's sister's daughter who is at the same time mother's brother's daughter insures this closeness of kinship, for then a man's successor will be his sister's son first and then his son's son. The Tlingit always speak with pride of having an opportunity of eventually passing the house on to their grandsons. This form of marriage combines matrilineal and patrilineal descent in the most direct way.

Rank is of supreme importance, and it, too, is insured by this form of marriage. A mother and a mother's brother are of the same rank, in the same way a father and a father's sister are of the same rank. Now, if your mother's brother is married to your father's sister, their daughter must be identical in rank with yourself, so this form of marriage correlates completely with the demand for equal status of mates.

House-group property cannot pass out of the house, for it regularly passes from mother's brother to sister's son. Individual property, however, can go out through a widow. Here, again, there are two different ways of checking this outflow. First, the Tlingit observe the levirate by which a man's widow goes to his younger brother. Thus if a woman is to go to her husband's brother who lives in the same house, the tendency is for her to keep the property and share it with her new husband. The levirate, therefore, effectively prevents property from going out of the house. Second, if there are no brothers left in the house, the widow theoretically goes to the oldest nephew. But, if she happens to be a mother-in-law of the nephew, which would be the case under the common form of marriage, she generally distributes the property among her own brothers. These brothers, however, are not far distant, for they are in the house of the mother's brother and also in the house where her own sons reside. Thus, if the levirate does not operate property is still kept within the close blood group. This group being made up of two intermarrying houses, property passes, in cases of this kind, back and forth between the two houses.

We can now sum up our study of the house-group with the following observation. Through the determining factors of descent, rank, marriage, and inheritance, we get a pairing of house-groups. These houses are of equal status and form close, intermarrying kin and property-owning groups. The reciprocity existing between the paired house-groups of opposing phratries works out in the following manner: (1) the young men are exchanged and marry the young women in the house to which they go, (2) bride gifts pass back and forth between these houses, (3) the individual property sometimes passes between these houses, (4) ceremonial duties are performed by the members of one house for the members of the other at birth; marriage; lip, ear, and nose piercing; house building; and burial. For these acts ceremonial gifts are given. Opposition in ceremonial activities takes places between these houses.

We thus get a picture of an entire Tlingit village through the examination of the behavior of two house-groups. What holds for the village, holds for the tribe. We see that, while matrilineal descent and inheritance form the basis of the kinship system, the Tlingit world is a thoroughly masculine one. Women own nothing but their clothes and ornaments and are only permitted to pass on their deceased husband's individual property. Women are, on the other hand, well treated, and socially they stand very high. They take part in all the ceremonies. Women are the means through which position, rank, and property flow from one generation to another, but they have no legal power to possess or use these privileges.

The Clan

We now come to the clan, a group of individuals living in a number of villages who identify themselves by using a common name, a number of crests, and who believe in a common local origin. Individuals composing a clan also believe themselves to be related through females and are an exogamic group. But as this is true of a greater group—the phratry—clan kinship and clan exogamy are thus derived and secondary. The clan acts as a whole only on rare occasions, such as when a feud of great dimensions occurs. The really important unit is the local division of the clan which acts as an integral part of the village. The clan, as a whole, has no chief and no common territory. The clan crests or emblems are often identified with the local division only. Whatever will be said here about the clan has specific reference to the local division. We shall approach the clan, first, from the point of view of internal structure, and then go on to study the relations of one clan to another. (For names, number, and ranking of clans, see Appendix.)

In our study of the house-group, we discovered the fundamental fact that through the marriage regulations, house-groups of opposing phratries became paired and made a close kin unit. It now remains to be seen what the kinship relations are between the different house-groups that form a local clan division.

During the migrations of the Tlingit clans, a number of house-groups of one clan would pick out a favorable spot and form a part of a village. Parts of other clans would follow and in this way a whole village would be established. The Klukwan division of the Ganaxtedi clan now have nine houses, only three of which can show genealogical relationship.

The relationship between these three houses can be historically verified, and their study throws considerable light on the effect of rank on house-groups in general. The original and, at that time, most important Ganaxtedi house was the Whale house. The Ganaxtedi clan was then, as now, the only Raven clan in Klukwan as opposed to three Wolf clans—the Kagwantan, and Šinkukedi, and the Daklawedi. The Ganaxtedi recognized no clan but the Kagwantan as their equal, and the Whale house matched itself only with the Killer-Whale's Fin house of the Kagwantan. Theoretically, there should have been no marriage outside of the Killer-Whale's Fin house, or at the most the Kagwantan. But individual preferences entered in and marriage with the other two clans occurred. It thus came about that the Whale house had within its walls Ganaxtedi-Kagwantan men and Ganaxtedi-Šinkukedi men, as well as Ganaxtedi-Daklawedi men. Matters of rank gave rise to serious disturbances within the Whale house, finally bringing about a situation in which the Ganaxtedi-Šinkukedi men set up a house for themselves, calling it the Raven house. The Ganaxtedi-Daklawedi men also left and called their new house the Frog house. The houses then ranked from the Whale house down to the Frog house. Members of these houses recognize their relationship and a considerable degree of cooperation exists between them. Thus, it seems that the house-groups of a village were both original units and also came to be by the splitting up of several original houses.

The ranking of the three Ganaxtedi houses is illustrative of the status of all houses within any clan. There is always one house which is of the highest rank, the rest of the houses being graded down to the lowest in rank. The three important houses of the Ganaxtedi marry with houses of equal rank in the Kagwantan of the opposite phratry. The Ganaxtedi houses of lower rank marry with the lower houses of the Kagwantan and with those of the Šinkukedi and Daklawedi.

The village clan division has hunting and fishing rights to certain carefully defined areas. Salmon streams are of considerable importance, and every clan has a number of these streams for its own use. These streams are often distantly separated from one another, and sometimes they are many days' journey from the winter villages. Claims to these salmon streams, in many cases, date from the migration when the clans had lingered temporarily at various places on their general movement northward. Hunting rights are usually taken to the watersheds of the salmon streams. Sealing islands off the coast and certain mountainsides for the hunting of mountain goats are special territories to which the clans lay claim through discovery. Within the village each clan has its portion of land upon which its houses are built. The leading house of the clan generally forms the center of such a unit. Patches of clover and other herbs, berries, trees, and regions where certain edible roots are plentiful are often owned by house-groups when they are situated near a village.

The local division of a clan does not participate in any productive activities as a unit. It does, however, take an active part in the preparation for a large potlatch. If a leading house proposes to give such a potlatch, it must get the consent of all house-groups of the local clan division. While one house is actually the sponsor and takes the responsibilities involved, each house is supposed to contribute its share of the property given away. It is, of course, understood by all that when a return potlatch is given a redistribution will take place.

In theory clansmen, in the old days, formed a group of considerable solidarity. Murder, when it occurred, was not punished within the clan. Theft, within the clan, did not occur. If adultery occurred, it was ignored. In fact, Tlingit women of high rank often had more than one husband, provided that both men belonged to the same clan. The subsidiary husband, once it was publicly known that he had relations with a certain woman, could not marry without her consent. It was the privilege of the woman to keep such a man and the husband could do little about it.

There were two crimes within the clan which were punished by death—witchcraft and incest. When a person was convicted of witchcraft, it was the duty of that person's clan to put him to death. Incest was also punished by the clan of the persons concerned. A clan could punish an individual who married much below his or her rank. It is said that marriage with a slave meant death to a person of high rank.

This clan solidarity is more apparent than real, for the element of rank is so strong that out of it crystallizes definite classes, the *anyeti* or noble class and the *x̱etax̱ua* or commoner class. Slaves, *gux̱*, of course, formed a third class, but they had no social rights and enter in only as a form of property. These class lines run across clan and phratry and form a unit probably stronger than the clan itself, for the *anyeti*, in each village at least, formed a kin group. In the village of Klukwan, the Whale, Raven, and Frog houses formed the *anyeti* of the Ganax̱tedi clan and also of the Raven phratry. The Killer-Whale's Fin house and the Bear house formed the *anyeti* of the Kagwantan clan and also of the Wolf phratry. The two other clans of the Wolf side had no houses important enough to be included in the noble class. Therefore, the *anyeti* in every village consists of the upper end of the two phratries, made up of the paired leading houses in the two highest clans. A member of the *anyeti* often ignores a clansman of low rank and does not speak of him as a brother, but as a man of such-and-such a house.

The relation of a division of a clan in one village to a division of the same clan in another village is not very clear but it seems to depend upon wealth. The Kagwantan of Klukwan were originally a branch of a large and powerful division of that clan at Sitka. The Klukwan division, through a series of able headmen, made themselves as important as the Ganax̱tedi clan of Klukwan and were finally accepted as of even higher rank than their clansmen at Sitka. The Klukwan branch of the Kagwantan took advantage of the trade routes into the interior and made themselves richer than the Sitka branch.

When the clans grew in numbers and class division became more accentuated, there was a tendency for them to split, one branch leaving for another region where it could establish itself by taking on a new name and crests. On being questioned, most Tlingit can tell one how these clans are related and what the specific dispute was that caused the break.

An important figure in the clan is the *ankaua* ("rich man"). The word chief does not fit the *ankaua* any more than it does the *yitsati* ("house-keeper"). The *ankaua* is not specifically the head of the clan, but he is the *yitsati* of the leading house. He is, therefore, the *yitsati* of highest rank. Theoretically, every clan has an *ankaua*, but owing to the ranking of clans only two *ankaua*s are recognized in each village, these being respectively the heads of the leading clans of the two phratries. And as the leading houses are paired, we often find that the two *ankauas* are father and son.

The element of generation enters into the succession of *ankaua*s. As already explained, leading houses of a clan form part of the *anyeti* or noble class, and are also a lineage which may occupy several houses. While there are differences of rank between the houses, these differences do not seem to override the importance of generation. Thus the *ankaua*-ship of the Ganaxtedi clan of Klukwan has, in the past thirty years, passed successively from the Whale house to the Raven house and then to the Frog house. At present, there are two brothers in the Frog house belonging to the older generation, and after the *ankaua*-ship has passed through the hands of both of these men it will go to the Raven house where the oldest nephew now resides. In a given house-group the *ankaua*-ship passes successively from the oldest to the youngest brother, then, instead of going to the sister's son in that house, it goes to the next oldest clan brother of that lineage regardless of what house he may reside in. Only after all the men of the brothers' generation have died does it go to the eldest son of any of the sisters. But at no time, in the leading clans at least, does it go out of the *anyeti* lineage.

The *ankaua* is a ceremonial leader and may represent the entire phratry at a village potlatch. On the other hand, however, when a clan has been invited to another village for a potlatch, then the *ankaua* represents only his own clan division. Even in these inter-village potlatches, lesser clans sometimes work with the leading clans of their own side.

The *ankaua* is not a war leader, but he takes an active part in all ceremonial matters concerning his clan. When clan disputes are to be discussed, the *ankaua* calls the various *yitsati* together and they hold a meeting in a sweat house, taking a steam bath and discussing clan affairs at the same time.

The *at'u²u* or totemic crests are intimately connected with the clan. While each phratry has one totem which is the common property of all the clans of that phratry, every clan has a number of subsidiary crests which belong expressly to that clan. In an analysis of the various clan crests there appears to be much duplication, but the duplication is only apparent, for while two clans may have a frog crest, the posture or shape of the frog is enough to differentiate the two. Also specific names differentiate the crests, such as killer-whale, killer-whale's fin, and the black killer-whale.

In the Raven phratry every clan may use the raven crest, which is given the highest symbolic form in the ceremonial hat. The raven hat of each local clan division is considered a separate entity, and if a clan division has more than one raven hat, these are considered separate and unequal in value. While the Raven phratry believed itself to be related to the culture hero Raven, the symbols of this totem now seem far removed from it. The Tlingit, in speaking of the raven emblems, mean specific hats, for each of which they have a specific name and valuation, and each stands for a house-group or a clan. The relationship between a crest and the mythical Raven is not now believed to exist.

Besides a principal crest, each clan has one or more emblems of lesser value. On the whole, the Tlingit have very few emblems as compared with the Haida and Tsimshian. The Tluk'naxadi, a Raven clan of Sitka, have the silver salmon and the cow as well as the raven as crests. The Kiksadi, also a Raven clan of Sitka, have the frog, the goose, the owl, and the sea lion cry. The Ganaxtedi of Klukwan have, besides the raven, the frog, woodworm, the black-skinned heron, and a large basket known as the Mother Basket. As to the crests belonging to the Wolf phratry, the Kagwantan of Klukwan have, besides the wolf, the eagle, the grizzly bear, the murrelet, and the killer-whale. The Naniyaya of Wrangell have the grizzly bear, the goat's head, and the shark in addition to the wolf.

A study of Tlingit totemism seems to lead to the conclusion that the totemic symbols correlate with the divisions in the social organization. Certain symbols identify the phratry, others the clan, and still others the house-group. Although the Tlingit call them all *at'u?u*, we can, for the sake of clarity, distinguish between the spiritual entity or totem, and the concrete symbol of that entity—the crest.

There seems to be a fundamental difference between the totemic systems of the Raven and the Wolf phratries. The clans belonging to the Raven phratry, which numbered about twenty-seven around the turn of the century, all use the raven in some form or other as their main emblem. They also relate it to the mythical Raven and they, themselves, claim to have come from the south and to be the first people to have settled in southeastern Alaska. In the Wolf phratry there is no such mythical unity. The wolf does not form the chief totem. In the south, the wolf is the main totem, but in the north the eagle is. In Klukwan and Sitka the people speak of themselves as Ravens and Eagles, in Wrangell as Ravens and Wolves. Another interesting fact is that the Wolf is not connected with a single definite mythical being comparable to the Raven. Legends show that the Wolf clans obtained their main crests through the individual experiences of clan members. The Raven clans accept their main crest by explaining it through a single origin. Furthermore, several groups of interior Athapascans have moved into Tlingit territory in historic times, and in every case they have been incorporated into the Wolf phratry.

While the Raven hat is connected with the mythical Raven, the subsidiary emblems and crests originate in the most curious ways. The cow of the Tluknakadi came to be an emblem of that clan when a cow hide prevented a pile of potlatch goods from getting wet. Another clan has the white man as a crest, for they believe they saw the white man before the other Tlingit. Then, again, ornaments and heirlooms of all kinds tend to become crests if they pass through a great number of potlatches. Displaying a pair of ear pendants increases their value at each successive potlatch until the pendants become a crest of that specific house-group which displays them and eventually of the entire clan division. The

Tlingit *yitsati* (photograph courtesy Thomas Burke Memorial Washington State Museum)

(*Top*) dancers at Klukwan potlatch; (*bottom*) dance shirt (photographs courtesy Thomas Burke Memorial Washington State Museum)

(*Above*) Klukwan girls with Chilcat blanket; (*left*) old totem pole at Wrangell

Old Tlingit women in canoe at Sitka

(*Top*) Klukwan village; (*bottom*) graveyard at Klukwan (photographs courtesy Thomas Burke Memorial Washington State Museum)

Mother Basket and the Worm Dish of Klukwan belong to this class of emblems, for the Mother Basket in particular was displayed merely as a large food basket originally, but it has been used so many time that its emblematic value is now very high. At betrothal, women of the *anyeti* class sometimes cut their hair and present it to the bridegroom's family; this hair is later displayed at the wedding ceremony and finally becomes an emblem of the bridegroom's clan. It seems, therefore, that the above-mentioned class of emblems commemorates certain important events in the lives of the clansmen. They seem to be only remotely connected with the supernatural, being more actual and historical in nature.

Besides these commemorative emblems, there are a number of emblems which deal with the supernatural experiences of certain clan members. Thus the frog emblem of the Kiksadi originated from a time in the past when a supernatural frog led the wandering clan to a spot which later became known as Sitka. The woodworm crest of the Ganaxtedi of Klukwan is also related to a past supernatural experience. The Naniyaya of Wrangell tell of a supernatural mountain goat which led a group of clansmen into safety after they had been lost in the mountains.

This brief sketch illustrates the differences in nature of the various objects used as emblems and crests and their relation to clan life. There seems to be a very definite connection between the raven emblems and the mythical origin of the entire Raven phratry, and its relations to the supernatural culture hero, Raven. The myths and crests of the Wolf phratry show no such unity.

We may speak of the phratry totems as primary, for the natives themselves always give them first place. The social function of these primary emblems or totems is undoubtedly to (1) differentiate one phratry from another, (2) give unity to its members, and (3) connect each of these groups to the external world.

In a second class we could put emblems that relate to the supernatural experiences of the mythical ancestors of the clan. At ceremonials these are generally given second place to the phratral totems. And finally, in a third class we could put the house-group crests, which in potlatches are given the lowest value. In our study of the consumption of wealth, the valuation and use of these totemic emblems and crests will become more clear. What has been attempted here is to point out that these symbols correlate with the social organization.

Every house, therefore, has a number of these sacred crests put away behind the screen and guarded by the *yitsati*. Clan emblems are generally kept in the house of the *ankaua*, but, as has already been pointed out, if the *ankaua*-ship shifts from one house to another the clan emblems, including the Raven hat, remain in one house which belongs to the *anyeti*. This house holds these emblems in trust, but permits any of the clan houses to display them at a ceremonial. After the ceremonial they are again returned to the house where they are stored. This house, therefore, forms a center of clan life and clan councils are held here.

Another interesting aspect of clan unity is the name system. Every clan has a number of socially valuable names that differ from birth names and nicknames. A man gets a personal name at birth which he keeps throughout his life, and this name is given to him by his uncle. When a nephew takes the place of his uncle, he is given one of the important honorific names of the clan. Through the means of rank and marriage, lineages have formed; and clan names, likewise, have become distributed among the various clan lineages and house-groups, with one group of names taking precedence over another

These names are intimately associated with the totem animals and their symbols. Like the totemic crests, these honorific names are relatively few and tend to be fixed in number. Like the crests, they are sacred and used only on ceremonial occasions. A man can take a new name only after emulating the ceremonial acts of some illustrious ancestor. At a potlatch only these names are used, and according to them the seating plan and the order of gift presentation are organized.

The correlations of names and emblems are made clear by the names themselves. The following are a number of honorific names belonging to the Ganaxtedi clan of Klukwan: Yełgok ("raven beauty"), Andakaneł ("flying raven"), Yełguxʷ ("raven slave"), Tanawak ("silver eyes"), Tłgina ("rustle of the raven's wings"), and Mustututsu ("putting two coppers together"). The Wolf names of the Kagwantan tell the same story: Anahoots (?"bear"), Guštetxanat ("free the slave, show the hat"), Gotšuxu ("wolf's teeth"), and Sauxšan ("gray-headed"—meaning the baldheaded eagle's head). Women also had personal and honorific names. The most common woman's name was formed by adding χa ("mother") to a man's name. Many women were thus known as mothers of such-an-such men, especially if they were of high rank and destined to bear sons with certain names. Besides these names were the honorific names for women, like Tonełtitušet ("crowded room"—referring to a ceremonial and potlatch), Tuwelihauxuxe ("giving more than the value"—meaning the value of slaves and coppers).

These examples show that the honorific names of men are connected with the totemic system and the giving of ceremonials. Women, on the other hand, are not permitted to use totemic names, and their honorific names related to potlatches and other social events.

When one looks over the names appearing in the genealogies, another important fact appears, for the honorific names tend to go in generations. A man takes the honorific name of his great-grandfather and, in turn, passes it on to his great-grandson. It is clear that this is a means for connecting the living with the dead. Just as the totemic symbols give unity to the clan and connect it to the world, so the name system gives continuity to the clan in time, tying the present to the past.

It must be added here that while most of the totemic symbols represent animals, birds, and fish, there is no intimate connection between these animate things and the totems. The totems, at any rate the chief ones, like the raven, wolf, eagle, and killer-whale, were mythical beings who could change from animal to human forms. The chief of these—the culture hero, Raven—did not create the world of men or animals, but made it possible for men to live happily. He obtained the sun from one spirit and the water to make the rivers from another. He freed the fish which were in a box far out in the ocean. The totems and emblems, even when they are represented by an animal, refer to spiritual entities. There are no taboos about killing the raven or any other bird or animal which is represented as a totem. The food collecting habits of the two phratries are the same. The raven and the eagle are not eaten but this is due to the low grade of flesh of these birds. The wolf is not eaten although it is hunted for its pelt. The black bear was eaten but the brown bear was hunted only for its pelt.

The Tlingit claim that the emblems of the Raven phratry represent animals, fish, and birds which are not killers, such as the raven, salmon, frog, woodworm, and mountain goat; and that those of the Wolf phratry represent killers, such as wolf, eagle, bear, and killer-whale. An analysis of the emblems reveals a number of inconsistencies in this dichotomy, but a Tlingit always explains this as being true to the pattern or else he ignores the question while still maintaining the principle of the dichotomy.

The Phratry

Within the village, phratries divide the people into two parts. While there were at least two villages which were made up of but one clan and phratry, the members of which married into another village, the great majority of the villages were made up of the two phratries. As the clan is made up in each village of a number of house-groups ranked in a series from the most important to the least important, so a phratry is made up of a number of clan divisions, similarly ranked from high to low. Taking a phratry as a whole, it is doubtful whether a perfectly ranked series of clans could be made. There are a number of clans in each phratry, each of which claims to be just as important as any other. We can say, therefore, that while there is only a rough grading of clans in a phratry as a whole, within each village the grading of clans is strictly adhered to.

Speaking of the whole phratry, we cannot say that it has any organized function, that is, its members do not act as an association. The clan, as a whole, is also weak, acting together only rarely in matters of feud and large scale potlatching. The phratry defines the marriage prohibitions, ceremonial labor, and ritual procedure, but outside of these general features, the phratry has little organized unity. What the phratry lacks in social action, it makes up somewhat in psychic unity, for all members of a phratry claim blood relationship with one another. The members of a phratry also claim to have certain psychic characteristics in common. The people of the Wolf phratry are considered warlike, quick-tempered, and restless wanderers; the Raven people are said to be wise, cautious, and the real founders of Tlingit society. The Tlingit themselves refer to the phratry as a tribe and claim that it is like Europe, made up of many different kinds of people often at war with one another.

This statement of the Tlingit is important because it reveals the extent of the lack of unity between the clans composing a phratry. In Tlingit law the clan is the ultimate source of political power. What the clan, especially its local division, decides is final in all disputes. These relationships are the same for clans within a phratry as they are for clans in opposite phratries. Some of the bitterest feuds were fought between clans of the same phratry. The loss of an individual through murder, the loss of property through theft, or shame brought to a member of a clan were clan losses, and the clan demanded revenge to an equal degree. That is to say, if a man of high rank was killed by a man of low rank in another clan, the murderer often went free while one of his more important kinsmen suffered death in his stead. Slight differences in rank could be overcome by payments of property, but the general demand in the case of murder was the life of a man of equal rank. In some cases where the offending clan was of lower rank, it was necessary to select a clan of the same phratry which could show some relationship to the offending clan, because none of the members of the offending clan could compensate for a crime committed against an important clan. But as this procedure was not theoretically established, a large scale feud might ensue. What was true of murder also applied to adultery and theft. If the adulterer was of higher rank than the husband of the woman concerned, he would generally go free, while his clan as well as the husband's clan paid the injured man a quantity of goods. If the adulterer was of equal rank or lower he would be almost certain to suffer death. Theft, if important, would be punished by death. But here again, the factor of status entered.

Every crime was considered a public delict. If a person was accidentally killed while hunting with individuals of another clan, his clan could demand a life from the clan with whom the man had been hunting. If a married man committed suicide because of his wife's behavior, the husband's clan could demand the life of a man of equal rank from the wife's clan.

In all legal disputes equality was the norm about which all restitution and indemnity centers. It was a life for a life of equal rank. If payments were made, then the value of a man was the bride gift of his mother. After a prolonged feud in which many lives were lost, both parties finally made peace by counting up their losses and settling the difference with payments of property.

Within the phratry, therefore, there is as little unity between the clans as there is between the members of the phratry considered as individuals. Within the village, however, the phratry theoretically acts as a ceremonial unit. While close relationship and rank cut across phratry lines and weaken this interphratral activity, there is still an attempt to maintain a semblance of unity. For instance, when ceremonial labor is performed, the people asked to do the work are a man's brothers-in-law, but any member of the opposite phratry may come around and take a hand in the work. When ceremonial gifts for this labor are made, the entire opposite phratry of the village is invited, feasted, and its members given gifts. The gifts given to the actual workers, however, are much larger than those given to the other members of the phratry. The same applies to all potlatch occasions. Both one's own phratry and one's opposite phratry are invited. The chief reason for this seems to be that the emblems displayed, the amount of gifts given, and the names taken have to be witnessed by everyone in the village.

We may now recapitulate what has been said about the social organization of the Tlingit. There are, first of all, the two important phratries that are the exogamic groups. In each of these phratries there were, until recently, over twenty clans, most of which had local divisions in two or more villages. Each local clan division is made up of a number of house-groups in each of which dwells a number of primary families. Descent and inheritance is reckoned through women.

This skeleton description, however, reveals little of the true nature of the social organization until we realize the operation of three fundamental forces, namely, rank, marriage, and wealth, upon it. Among the Tlingit these three factors are of supreme importance and it would be exceedingly difficult to say which of them was primary—to say which the cause, which the effect. All that we can truly say is that these factors give Tlingit society its peculiar form. There is pairing of clan divisions and house-groups in each village leading to the formation of lineages and classes which cut across the clan and phratry and weaken their solidarity.

Wealth gives Tlingit society, in common with other Northwest Coast societies, its characteristic means to the ends sought. War as an organized means to individual and group eminence did not occur. When legal means fail, the feud is resorted to, but in the end it, too, is settled legally by all losses being weighed one against the other and property payments smoothing over the ir-regularities which still remain. The important man among the Tlingit is not a warrior in the sense in which this is true among the Plains Indians; nor is he a shaman trafficking with the spiritual powers as is true of the Indians of Washington and Oregon; nor, again, is he a priest supplicating the spirits to bring favors to his people as is true of the Pueblo Indians. The important men among the Tlingit—the *yitsati* and the *ankaua*—are men who seek to raise their lineage, their house-group, and their clan to honor and eminence through the accumulation, display, and disposal of ma-terial wealth. This process of using wealth will be treated fully in a later chapter.

This brings us to the pre-eminently meaningful element in Tlingit culture—their totemism or crest system, as it has been variously called. We have just said that the important Tlingit is not a priest in the usual sense of the word. While the emblems are connected with the supernatural and the mythical past, these beings, such as the Raven, the Wolf, and the Eagle, are not wor-shipped. They are never prayed to. They explain and account for the existence of the Tlingit world. If a Tlingit wishes super-natural power he seeks it through a shaman, but the spirits thus sought are in a different category. The Tlingit does not believe that the Raven, the Wolf, and the Eagle, as mythical beings, exist today. All that is left of this mythical period is the body of sym-bols, and it is these symbols themselves that the Tlingit deem sacred. They are his link with order and meaning in the universe, his explanation of natural and social phenomena.

These symbols also have another function, that of integrating the group to which they belong and also of elevating that group above its competitors. Along with these material symbols go the honorific names which maintain the continuity of the group in time. This identity between the group and the symbols makes these symbols the ready mark of the group or of the leader of the group. If there is a change in the relation of one group to another, it is correlated with a change in the symbols of that group. Therefore, to make one's group important is equivalent to making one's symbols important, and the accredited means for raising one's group, and incidentally one's self, is the giving away of wealth. The full details of this procedure will be dealt with later. What has been attempted here is the correlation of the system of symbols with the world and the social group, and the group and its social activities.

The House

Still another matter of importance is the Tlingit house. We have seen how the totemic crests relate man and the world, and how the name system provides a temporal unity, but we have not yet shown what provides the spatial relationship of the Tlingit to the world about them. The Tlingit house can be considered the prime symbol of Tlingit culture, not only in its spatial relationship, but also in its mythical relationship. Territory does not seem to have a sacred significance to the Tlingit. Clans take up hunting and fishing territories wherever they happen to go, and clan legends reveal many changes in the location of the clan divisions. What is true of territory is also true of the food supply. There is no ritual, no ceremonialism connected with fish, nor the food animals and the processes of catching them. There is, of course, the mythical beliefs connected with the origin of the physical world and the objects in it. Moreover, there is magic concerned with individual activities, but group ceremonialism does not appear in connection with the food supply and the principal economic processes. Furthermore, in the old days, the dead were burnt and their ashes placed inside of the sacred totem poles. At no time, in his pagan days, would a Tlingit consider putting his dead in the profane earth. In fact, a Tlingit thinks with terror of being drowned or of being lost in the woods. The spirit of a person so lost does not go to join the ancestors, but becomes a *kuštaka* and wanders about forever, haunting the living with his doleful cries.

But, as has already been explained, house building is through and through a ceremonial activity. Only men of the opposite phratry can build one's house. Slaves used to be sacrificed in the post holes. The tearing down of an old house, the building of a new one and its opening are all accompanied by ceremonialism. Furthermore, a house has a fixed position in a village and it cannot be moved to another place, for it would not then be the same house. If the house is too small, annexes are built and even separate houses, but these are still parts of the same house and have but a single name. The house-group is a definite social entity and the house is its external manifestation in space.

Social life and social values center in the house, which is sacred. The name of the house is totemic and remains the same no matter how many times the house is rebuilt. The house posts are carved with all the emblems and crests which the house possesses. The screen or *nahen* is likewise painted with the crest symbols and hides that part of the house which is the repository for the sacred ceremonial symbols and is the private place of the *yitsati* who himself becomes sacred on ceremonial occasions. The round opening in the screen emits the *yitsati* at rituals as if he were born again from the mythical regions of the past. The doorway and house front, too, are carved with the crest animals to identify the house for a visitor. The much talked of totem poles were originally within the house, and not until historic times, when steel tools made it possible to increase their size, were they moved outside in front of the house. Even today, the totem pole is considered part of the house.

The house is never so intimately connected with the woman as it is with the man. A woman, through marriage, often lives in a strange house and is not supposed to understand the meaning of the symbols of her husband's house. Childbirth is a profane act and a woman must be removed to a small temporary hut outside the house where she gives birth. At puberty, on the other hand, a girl is considered sacred and is kept concealed behind the screen so that she cannot see the sea or hunting and fishing gear or the ordinary processes of life. It is at this period that her lower lip is pierced, that she becomes a member of society. Her debut from seclusion becomes the occasion of a great potlatch and rejoicing on the part of her relatives.

The transfer of a boy from his father's house to his uncle's house in a way constitutes an initiation, for it is in this latter house that he is introduced to his social group. Small boys are presented by their uncles to guests on every ceremonial occasion; they wear ceremonial articles at potlatches and behave as adult members of society. Uncles begin to present their nephews with honorific names while they are still quite young. We can thus say that a boy is a member of a clan and of society the moment he steps into his uncle's house. This is true also because the house is sacred and the sacred symbols and knowledge are always there influencing the mental development of the boy. Among the Tlingit, there are no secret societies, no secret rites for initiations for boys other than those connected with shamanism.

All social affairs of a ritual nature, too, take place in the house which, in turn, is intimately connected with the fundamental group of society, namely, the house-group. A man is educated, married, and gives the great potlatches of his life in his own house. When he dies, his body is placed in a sitting posture before the ceremonial opening in the screen, while his clansmen and his opposites feast and rejoice about him. Later his ashes are put into a cavity in a totem pole so that his spirit will join the ancestors in the hills back of the village. But through the sacred emblems and names he is still part of the community, and food is put into the fire at each potlatch so that the dead ancestors can enjoy it, for they are taking part in the proceedings going on in the sacred house—the center of the Tlingit world.

III

PROPERTY

In the preceding chapter the question of property was touched upon in connection with the social groups and the principal individual relationships established by matriliny, rank, and marriage. I now wish to treat this subject more fully in order to bring out the fundamental correlations of Tlingit ownership. Property, as here understood, is the sum of the rights of individuals to the disposal of objects of social value. In analyzing Tlingit property relationships, I wish to answer three questions: (1) What is owned and by whom? (2) How are property rights acquired? (3) How are these rights validated?

Clan property in the old days consisted of salmon streams, hunting grounds, berry patches, sealing rocks, house sites in villages, rights to passes into the interior (see discussion in Chapter VII), certain important totemic crests, and shamanistic spirits. It must be emphasized that the local clan division is the primary owning group. While any member of a clan may use the resources belonging to a local clan division, he generally expects to be invited to do so.

The acquisition of new fishing streams and hunting grounds is very closely correlated with the pressure of population determined by physical environment and technology. The Tlingit speak of a constant drift northward from the mouths of the Nass and the Stikine rivers. For a long time a number of clans would remain near a certain river. Then quarrels over women and wealth would split the village, one portion going off in search of new territories. These quarrels over wealth arose in connection with the bride gifts and potlatches. But as wealth came originally through fishing, hunting, and trading, those in possession of the poorer resources had to seek new regions for exploitation. It is conceivable that disputes over property rights could be settled by making the necessary legal adjustments. But when new resources were within easy reach, it was probably simpler to move on to a new region while still retaining the old social relationships and rank.

New grounds were acquired through conquest or settlement on virgin territory, or by agreement to share certain large areas with other clans. As the Tlingit moved northward, they constantly met settlements of Athapascans who had come down the rivers to the coast. The Tlingit either drove the Athapascans away or mingled with them. Klukwan was an Athapascan village some eight generations ago. When suitable uninhabited places were found, the Tlingit would give the spot a name and settle there. A single clan, owing to the dual organization, found it difficult to function if it lived far from the clans of the opposite side. It was customary for a clan, taking up a new site, to invite members of some opposite clan to come and live in its village, these people generally being fathers or brothers-in-law.

In places where a number of clans live together, the allocation of resources correlates very closely with the principle of scarcity. When a number of clans settled on the banks of large rivers, like the Stikine, Taku, and Chilcat, the question of rights to salmon fishing did not arise. There was plenty for everyone in the large river. Similarly deep sea fishing was unrestricted by property rights. But on the islands the rivers were smaller and the important ones far apart. It was thus necessary to apportion the resources in some manner. The local clan units were of a size to subsist on the supply of these smaller rivers. In fact, there is a very close correlation between the size of the local clan units and their resources. Large clans often held a good sized stream while the tributaries were taken over by the smaller clan divisions.

The size and nature of the village is also directly influenced by the quantity and movements of the various species of salmon. The large rivers, with their abundant and constant water supply, provided spawning beds for many kinds of salmon which came at different times of the year. The sockeye came in July and remained until October; the king, humpback, and dog salmon began to run in September and remained in the rivers until December; the silver salmon or coho did not enter the rivers until November and December and remained until February. The steelhead salmon and the Dolly Varden trout came in February or as soon as the river began to rise enough to allow them room to swim, and they remained until April and May. Thus the mainland rivers were supplied with fish practically the year around. In conformity with this certain food supply we find large villages on the banks of these rivers, from which the people moved only in May to make fish oil out of the eulachon which crowded the mouths of the rivers.

On the islands, the village was primarily the winter residence, where the people depended upon deep sea fishing. In July, each local clan division would move to its salmon stream and not return until November. In regions where salmon were scarce, the Indians became expert seal hunters, and we find a threefold division of settlement. In March when the weather began to clear, the various clan units would go to the rocks and islets far out to sea and spend the entire spring there, living on seal meat, deep sea fish, shellfish, and sea birds' eggs. In July they would move to their salmon streams, and in November the clan divisions would be united for four months in their winter villages. These villages were usually situated in quite sheltered spots, and the great ceremonials of the year were held in them. Hence, with a certain technological system the Tlingit had to adjust themselves, in different regions, to the varying conditions of their food supply. This, in turn, affected the allocation of resources, the modes of settlement, and the conceptions of property.

Within the village the clan divisions had sections of ground which belonged to them alone. This territory was divided up among the house-groups of the clan for house sites and burial places. In Klukwan, where the village still retains its old form, we can see how the order of settlement and rank of the clans have affected the form of the village. The Ganaxtedi, who claim to be the original settlers, have the best part of the river bank and are now in the center of the village. The Kagwantan have settled on both sides of the Ganaxtedi. The Šinkukedi and the Daklawedi, both small in number and low in rank, have settled, one on each end of the village. (See Map 1.)

In former days, the funeral pyres, where the bodies of the

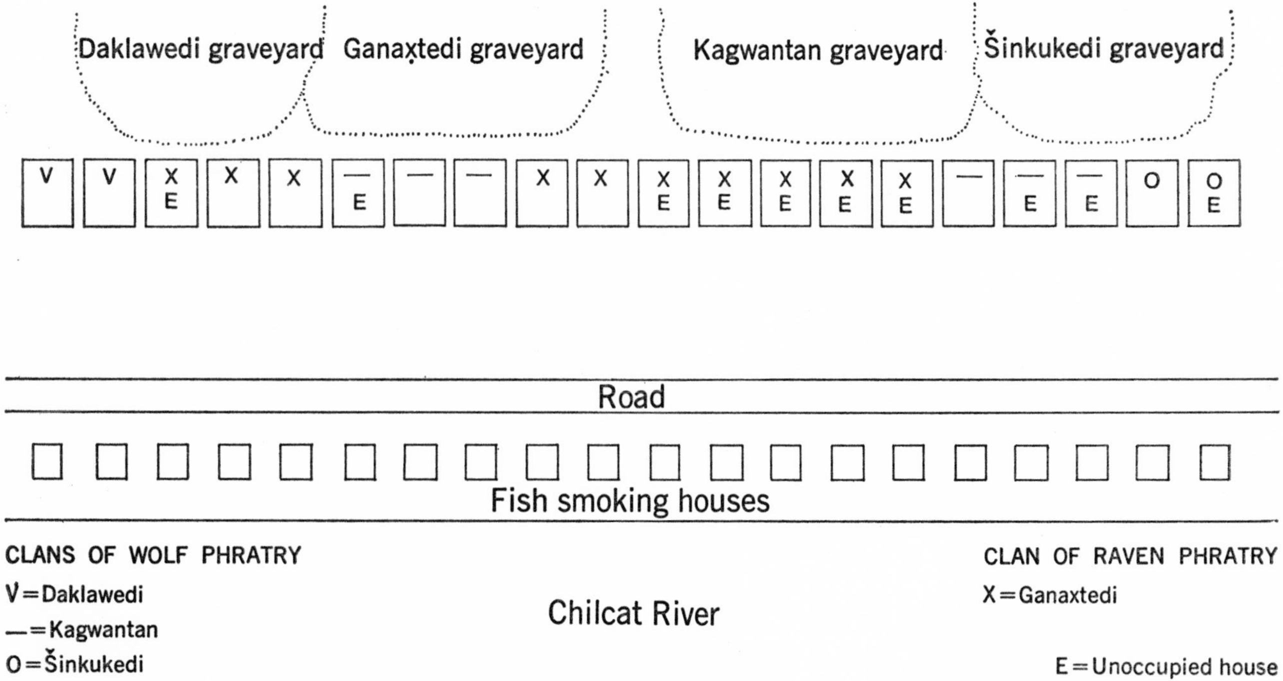

Daklawedi graveyard   Ganaxtedi graveyard   Kagwantan graveyard   Šinkukedi graveyard

| V | V | X E | X | X | — | — E | — | X | X E | X E | X E | X E | X E | — | — E | — | O | O E |

Road

Fish smoking houses

Chilcat River

CLANS OF WOLF PHRATRY

V = Daklawedi
— = Kagwantan
O = Šinkukedi

CLAN OF RAVEN PHRATRY

X = Ganaxtedi

E = Unoccupied house

Map 1. Plan of Klukwan village

dead were burnt, were situated at the back of the clan house sites. A small clan would have one, a large clan might have several. The poles in which the ashes of the important men were deposited stood before the houses. The Tlingit are now Christians and each clan has its own burial ground immediately back of its house sites. The totem poles, which are hewn from stone by gravestone makers in Seattle, are placed over the graves. The Tlingit takes advantage of the white man's heaven, but he still remains a member of his own clan, and holds on to its crests and burial sites.

The question of boundaries gave little trouble. The salmon streams, when small, were owned throughout their length; when large, as we have seen, the question of ownership did not enter. The hunting grounds usually consisted of the watershed of the streams or valleys well enclosed by hills or high mountains. In Klukwan, the clans divided the mountain slopes for goat hunting by the Ganaxtedi taking the valley above the village and the Kagwantan taking the valley below the village. The other two clans had valleys in the more distant tributaries of the main stream. Berry, root, and clover patches were small and often possessed by single houses. The same was true of rocks for sealing.

In the allocations of territories, the agreements as to the boundaries and their permanent acceptance were constantly influenced by the power of the stronger clans and the factor of kinship. It usually worked out that the strongest clans had the nearest and best sources of supply and that they steadily infringed upon the rights of the weaker if this were worthwhile. The expansion of the Kagwantan was at the expense of the Šinkukedi and Daklawedi. The expansion of the Ganaxtedi was at the expense of the Ganaxati, a clan living some five miles below the village. The Ganaxtedi, for some reason which I was unable to discover, wished to have the territory occupied by the Ganaxati, and, therefore, drove them out. This was done by laying claim not to their territory but to their totemic crests. After a long feud, what remained of the Ganaxati left the entire region which is now claimed by the Ganaxtedi. The Ganaxtedi, on the other hand, got along well with the Kagwantan with whom they intermarried and maintained close kinship ties. And, as already mentioned, close relatives were invited to settle in the village.

Rank is even more important than numerical power and kinship ties in determining the distribution of clan settlement and clan territories. Men who marry women of higher rank than themselves from other villages have sons whose rank is that of their mothers. Theoretically these sons should go to reside in the village of their mother's brother. This is generally done and the eldest son remains as the heir of this maternal uncle. But every inducement is made by the father's clan to get the boys to come back and settle in their father's village when they have grown up. Not only do the fathers wish to have their eminent sons near them, but the whole clan wishes to have marital, ceremonial, and economic relations with a clan of high rank. Thus the principle of rank works in opposition to the principle of residence demanded by maternal descent, and other clans are keen to note this discrepancy when it conflicts with their interests. New clan divisions must be given property in house sites and hunting and fishing grounds, and, if they are of high rank, the best available territories are sought. The Kagwantan who are of high rank came to Kukwan through marriage and have gradually gained many of the hunting valleys formerly possessed by the Sinkukedi. Today, although the clan organization has very little force, it is used in claims to property, both maternally and paternally. If it is most advantageous to be connected with your father, you choose him rather than your uncle. Kagwantan men were found trapping in Ganaxtedi property and, when asked why they had the right, replied that their father had invited them to do so. Other villages claimed that they should not be there but, as their father was an important man, nothing could be done about it.

With the introduction of firearms, steel traps, and the great demand for furs, a new orientation was given to Tlingit production. Trapping had always been an individual enterprise, for it supplied a man, his wife, and their children with the necessary parts of their dress and bedding. But as compared with the collective activities of fishing, hunting, and the acquisition of moose and caribou hides, trapping for furs was of lesser importance. The coming of the fur trade disturbed this balance. The individual activity of trapping was now given a central place in the economy. Individuals built permanent lodges in their clan territory where they resided every winter for months at a time. With the intensification of fur hunting, the fur-bearing animals began to lessen in number with the consequence that the formerly un-divided clan territories began to be cut up into small sections, to each of which an individual laid claim. The group most acutely affected by this change in production was the house-group. Its economic unity was shattered. Collective activities diminished in importance with the increase in individual wealth and purchasing power. What is of importance here is to show how property relationships can be affected by a change in the methods of pro-duction. A group formerly collective in its principal economic enterprises becomes individualistic in production accompanied by the parceling out of an original undivided territory.

The next areas to be discussed are the rights to noneconomic forms of property, such as the totemic crest and spirits. In dis-cussing totemism, it was pointed out that each clan had one or more crests which took the form of hats or other carvings. These clan crests were the common property of the clan and could be used by any of its members. These crests usually belonged to the houses of the clan whose members were the *anyeti* (noble class) and who came to identify themselves and their crests with the entire clan. The correlation of these crests with rank and wealth will come out more clearly in the discussion of the potlatch. The spirits invoked by the shaman were often claimed by clans, as pointed out in Chapter I, but this claim was not always legally sanctioned. With these spirits, as with the totemic crests, there always went a number of names, songs, dances, and stories which were limited to the claimants of the spirits.

The village, as a whole, had very little unity. It was defended only against the attacks of other than Tlingit Indians. Tlingit warfare consisted in clan feuds and quite often, when a clan would come to attack that part of a village where its enemies dwelt, the other clans would stand by as observers or would exhort the fighters to stop and settle the matter with payments of goods or slaves.

The village had, however, a road which passed between the houses and the river bank or beach and a stream from which drinking water was obtained. While the clans each looked to their section of the road, the water supply was everyone's con-cern and it was kept clean by common consent. When trails led to other villages, they had sometimes to be cleared of snow and landslides. The usual custom was to make a trail around the obstruction, but often a number of men interested in getting through would clear up the old trail. This was, however, a temporarily organized activity. The beach was generally common property, but a clan could claim the waterfront immediately before its house sites. In Klukwan, in the old days, there were sporadic attempts by all the clans to build large weirs in the Chilcat River. The undoubted economic advantage of this type of cooperation, demanding large numbers of men, was seen by the Indians, but the friction between the clans continually broke down the enterprise. The salmon trap would be built under the impulse of the initial enthusiasm of some intelligent person but, when constant repairs were needed, the question of dividing up the work proved too difficult to resolve. Dividing the catch also caused some altercation and after several years the weir would break down and the clans would go back to their former fishing enterprises.

The house-group owned the house, slaves, large canoes, important tools and food boxes, important weapons, ceremonial gear, and the food products of collective work. As pointed out in the preceding chapter, these objects were held in trust by the *yitsati* ("keeper of the house") for the use of the group as a whole or one of its members. The functions of house-group property are best seen by contrasting house-group property with individual property, which consists of tools, weapons, small canoes, clothing, decorations, and ceremonial objects.

The climate of Tlingit country demanded a good shelter. Long cold winters, strong winds, and rainfall made it imperative that a Tlingit have a good house. Each man could have built a house for himself and his wife as is done by natives in so many parts of the world. Why should a group like the Tlingit house-group be a house-owning body? There is a strong connection with the difficulties involved in making a house out of wood. With stone tools, trees are difficult to fell, and it took months to split and hew the necessary posts and planks. The decoration of the posts, plates, and moldings also required much time and skill. Thus the heavy costs involved in the making of a house made it more economical for a group of close relatives, like brothers and their sisters' sons, to band together to accumulate enough wealth to build a house. Large canoes were used by the house-group as a whole in traveling and were made and owned by the group as a whole. It is needless to enumerate all the objects, for all that correlate with collective enterprise are collectively owned.

Small tools, weapons, food, and clothing in use, are individually owned for sound economic reasons which it is unnecessary to elaborate here. The relationship of group need to individual need is seen in the ownership of firearms when they first came into use. The high cost of flint locks was prohibitive to the individual who formerly used his private spear and bow and arrow. The house-group purchased those articles, and the *yitsati* kept them in store until a large hunt or feud was decided upon. With the increase of private wealth through trapping, individuals gradually came to possess guns. What was to be owned and by whom depended, therefore, primarily upon the importance of the objects in the satisfaction of needs, and upon their scarcity and cost. These primary factors were constantly affected by the forces exerted by kinship, rank, and individual self-seeking.

To privately owned objects an individual gets his right through production, exchange, and inheritance. The requisition of objects through individual effort will be treated under production (Chapter IV) and distribution (Chapter VI), and enough has been said about both individual and group property in social organization to show how closely they are bound up with the rest of the culture. What needs to be described now are the sanctions by which these property rights are validated.

Clan membership, determined by maternal descent, establishes the local relationship of an individual to clan property. Adoption into a clan is not known. This legal relationship or property right is binding to the extent that the whole social conception of the clan stands behind it. All members are bound by common consent to defend clan property against outside encroachments, to share the use of their property as agreed upon by themselves, and to see that no individual member transgresses the defined rules set by tradition and enforced by economic expediency. Alienation takes place only when clan membership is lost through witchcraft or incest. The exchange of clan property is against all principles of clan unity and never occurred in the old days. In more recent times, the Taku clans are said to have rented their fishing rights to other clans, but this is undoubtedly due to white influence. Today, with the breakdown of ceremonial life, the clans have sold or are rapidly selling their ceremonial gear to museum collectors and curio hunters, sharing the payments among themselves. The old men look sadly on these sales and demand that the sacred articles be buried with them when they die.

Besides the legal rights to territories set up by clanship, there is the sanction of mythology. Every clan has a legend of how its ancestors were led to their present village by supernatural aid and were advised to remain there. The totem animals or birds appeared and led the way into favorable inlets and rivers. The story of the Kiksadi clan of Sitka is typical of these legends (Swanton 1909). It relates how the Kiksadi had been wandering northward for several years, never certain as to where to establish a village. One day, when they were off Sitka Sound in a dense fog, a frog appeared and circled about the canoes for some time, then started toward the land. The canoes followed and were led by the frog into Sitka harbor where the Kiksadi were overjoyed to find a pleasant village site. The frog was then taken as the crest of the Kiksadi clan.

When house-groups broke up, the discontented members built a house of their own, giving it a name and a crest acquired through a supernatural experience. The spirits of the dead also lived in clan hunting and fishing grounds, coming to the village only on ceremonial occasions. The great rivers of Tlingit country, the fish, and the sunlight were secured for the Tlingit by their culture hero, Raven. Property relationships, among the Tlingit, while formed by economic considerations, are made binding by the legal sanctions of their social organization and the religious sanctions embodied in their mythology.

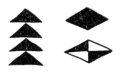

IV

THE ANNUAL CYCLE OF PRODUCTION

Among the Tlingit the cycle of production consists of three classes of activities: collecting, storing, and manufacturing. The term collecting is here used in the broader sense to include hunting, fishing, berry picking, and root, bark, seed, and herb gathering. Storing consists in the preparation and preservation of foods for consumption in periods in which they cannot be gathered. Manufacturing consists in the handicrafts, the activities which supply clothing, shelter, technical equipment, and ceremonial articles. As these activities are closely connected with seasonal changes they will be studied from month to month. As this temporal pattern varies from one place to another in the region occupied by the Tlingit, the more striking variations will be indicated.

The Tlingit year begins with the July moon. This is the month when the great schools of salmon first appear in the rivers, when the period of abundant and easily obtained food supply begins. But the economic year begins in March, the month in which the food collection activities commence.

Kašaka (March). This month tends to be stormy with strong westerly and southwesterly gales accompanied by sleet and rain. The days are quite long and the Tlingit fisherman feels both the monotony of a dried fish diet and the restrictions of the village. For some weeks now he has had his lines and hooks ready and has seen to his canoes. They have been drawn down to the beach from their brush shelters near the smoke houses, and their bottoms have been seared clean of slivers with a pine torch. Good luck amulets have been hidden in the bows, and the paddles have been trimmed. Everyone feels the urge of spring and excitement rules the village.

On the islands this is the month for halibut and cod fishing. On the mainland, while cod and halibut are caught in the inlets, trout fishing forms a more important activity. Now, of course, steel hooks and cotton lines are used in fishing, but in the old days, the wooden hook with a bone barb and a cedar bark, kelp, or rawhide line were used.

The fishermen, in the old days, would use either a single hook or a score of hooks, attached to a mainline, about six feet apart. At both ends he fastened heavy stones for sinkers. This line with the hooks attached would be lowered by another line, to the upper end of which would be fastened a distended seal's bladder to mark the place where the line was lowered. These lines were baited with clams or bits of fish already caught and taken some miles out to sea where sand and mud banks were known to be. Here the fishermen would lower a number of lines, let them remain for half a day or so, and then draw them up. As the fish were brought to the surface, the fishermen would dispatch them with a blow from a decorated fish club and toss them into a large basket in the center of the canoe.

Single hook fishing was practiced close to the shore. The more lines used, the more men were required. Often all the men of the house-group would go out and camp on the small islands and rocks. These distant fishing trips were the most dangerous enterprises, and many tales are told of narrow escapes and of the supernatural help gotten by the fishermen of old.

When the fish are brought home, the women take charge of them. Some are boiled or broiled for immediate consumption, and others are given as gifts to relatives. The remainder are split down the back, the vertebrae are removed, and the fish are hung on long poles to dry in the sun or are cured in the smoke houses. It is a happy day when the fishermen return both for the women and children and for the hungry dogs who sit by waiting for the backbones and heads.

In March the mainland rivers open up and, when the ice disappears, the fisherman takes his gill-net and makes drifts down the river. In the old days, rawhide and cedar bark twine were used for making these nets with bladders for floats and stones for sinkers. The fish would endeavor to go through the net and would get caught in the meshes by their gills. Two men usually operated a canoe, one paddling, the other handling the net. The commonest trout was the Dolly Varden although rainbow and cut-throat were often caught. Trout were eaten fresh, the weather being still cold enough to keep the fish for a week. They were thrown on the snow on the roofs of the houses, out of the reach of dogs.

Shellfish are at their best in March. On the islands great quantities of clams and mussels are taken and dried, smoked, and packed in airtight boxes or hung in the roof where they keep dry. The mainland tribes had to trade dried meat or hides for these shellfish of the islands. One of the great delicacies of the old days was clams baked in an oven. A hole was dug in the ground and lined with stones. A fire was built in it and removed when the stones were hot. A layer of wet leaves was then put down. The clams were placed on the leaves and covered with another thick layer of leaves. Periodically water was poured over them. After six hours the clams would be baked, and the whole house-group would sit around to a feast.

When the Tlingit trapped for his own use only, he did it in March. Midwinter was too cold and the snow too deep for comfortable travel. Deadfalls were set for the wolf, fox, mink, and otter. Sea otter would be hunted with the spear, several canoes surrounding it out at sea. Bear dens would be looked for in the autumn or winter and marked so that late in March, when the bears began to stir from their dens, the Indians were ready to catch them before they became too strong. Many men armed with spears and as many dogs as possible set forth to drive the bear from his den. When the animal was a large Alaskan brown bear, the undertaking was dangerous. The strength and ferocity of these bears is well recognized even today among the expert hunters. The dogs would worry the half-awakened bear until he came to the mouth of the den, where men with spears would be ready for him. Some would stand over the entrance of the den and, as the bear came out, would try to spear it in the head and neck. Often they would succeed only in wounding the bear which made it attack them. A furious battle then ensued in which a number of dogs were always killed and sometimes even men. Seldom did the hunters escape without cuts and bruises from the paws of the huge animal. Pits and deadfalls were also used in the past, but today powerful steel traps are set for the bear. The flesh of the bear was poor in spring and was eaten by the dogs. The pelt, however, was in its prime and was carefully scraped and dried for use as a robe or a rug.

Tšinkada (April). Deep sea fish and trout continue in this month, but the storage of deep sea fish diminishes as other activities begin to occupy more time. Seaweeds of various kinds are collected by the women, brought home in large baskets, dried in the sun, chopped up, and packed in airtight boxes. In the mainland river valleys some trapping goes on for mink, muskrat, and marten, but on the islands the hair of the fur bearing animals deteriorates rapidly with the approach of warm weather.

Rabbits are snared with a spruce root loop. Porcupines are killed with a stick as they cannot escape man. If one climbs a tree, the hunter will follow it and shake it from the branch while another will club it when it hits the ground. Marmots are dug out of their holes on the mountainsides, their pelts and flesh both being valuable.

As the snow and ice disappear, the ducks and geese begin to return from the south, and the old hunters prepared arrows with many points which they shot into a large flock of feeding ducks. If the ducks were too far from the shore, the hunters would cover a canoe with branches and approach the flock slowly until they were near enough to shoot into it. Ducks were also hunted at night by torchlight. When they were known to feed in narrow ditches, nets were spread over these ditches, and as the ducks passed under them both ends were dropped and the ducks captured.

In April, the large blue grouse begin to hoot on the hillsides, making it easy to locate them. The birds live on birch buds and are very fat and lazy and permit one to come near enough to shoot them with a bow and arrow. The male willow grouse drums and lets the hunter know of his whereabouts. While drumming he is oblivious to his surroundings and can often be knocked over with a stick.

Tšinkadunaxa (May). Spring is now in full swing. Dawn breaks at half-past two in the morning and daylight lasts until eleven at night. There is a tremendous surge in plant life. In the pleasant weather people go out in search of green plant foods, like the tender stems of the salmonberry, wild rhubarb, and wild clover. The young people often stay on the islands and headlands where these plants are abundant, camping at night in brush and bark shelters. Most of the green plants are consumed at once, for the body has been starving for them.

Many varieties of roots are collected by the women, boiled, dried, and packed away for the coming winter. The bark of the hemlock is peeled off, and the soft white cambium layer is scraped into boxes, cooked, pressed into cakes, and stored. Deep sea fishing and hunting are carried on only for immediate consumption.

May is the month when immense quantities of fish oil are prepared. On the islands herring are caught with a herring rake, a long pole with a row of spikes on one end. The herring school so thickly that when the rake is pushed through the water the herring are impaled upon it. A line with many hooks is also let down and then jerked up quickly, the fish sticking to the hooks. The herring come to spawn in shallow water, despositing their eggs on seaweed or anything that may be convenient. Thousands of them are left on the beach by the ebbing tide where they can be collected by the Indians. If hemlock boughs are put into the water for an hour or so they will become covered with herring roe. The bough is then placed in boiling water and when the eggs are cooked they are eaten off the bough.

By far the most important oil fish is the eulachon, an extremely fat fish about four inches in length. In May, these fish crowd the mouths of the large rivers for the purpose of spawning, and the Indians for miles around gather to catch them and to reduce them to oil. The eulachon is caught with a small dip net. To a hoop about three feet in diameter, a cone-shaped net is attached, the bottom of which is opened and closed by means of a string. While one man guides the canoe, the other dips the net among the closely packed fish swarming around the boat. The net full of fish is deposited in the boat by opening the hole in the bottom of the net. It is then closed for the next dip.

When a canoe load of fish is brought to the shore, the women and old men put them into canoes which have been cleaned for the purpose. Fresh water is poured in and then heated stones are used to bring the fish to a boil. After several hours of boiling the mass is permitted to settle and cool. The oil is then skimmed off the surface of the water with large horn spoons and stored in seal bladders. The old people believed that if the fish were allowed to decay a little the oil would be better. As it is, the oil very quickly gets rancid and has a repulsive odor. The oil is not only eaten with most foods but is used for preserving berries, roots, and herbs and is drunk at feasts in large quantities.

Toward the latter part of May, when the oil is made and most of the early storage activities are finished, the house chiefs, in former days, went on trading expeditions. The people at the heads of the rivers went inland and used fish oil as one of their chief articles. The people of the coast went down to the Haida and Tsimshian for the large cedar canoes, taking Chilcat blankets with them as trade goods.

Tšinkadunaxadixa (June). No storage activities mar the pleasures of the Indians in this month. What fishing, hunting, or gathering is done is for direct consumption. Berries begin to ripen; roots and herbs are eaten. The people spend days on the islets off the coast eating the eggs of the sea birds.

This is also a time of fine weather, and potlatching takes place. Houses are built in this month. The timbers have been prepared in the winter and now, in the fine weather, the men of the other phratry put up the house. Trading started in May and is carried on throughout June. All long voyages are made for the days are long and the winds tend to be westerlies, blowing during the day and dying down at night.

Tlexa (July). This month is the turning point in the year. The great schools of salmon that spawn in the rivers of Alaska now begin to crowd the estuaries and the mouths of the rivers, struggling to get into quiet pools where they can deposit their eggs and sperm and then die. This regular appearance of a bountiful and certain food supply gives stability and permanence to the life of the Tlingit. Although a fisherman and a hunter, he does not need to roam far. From the large permanent villages he can easily go to the streams to gather in his annual harvest of salmon. But this harvest does not begin in July, and the Indian is satisfied to eat the fresh eggs, going out every other day to bring in a supply. It is a time of ease and pleasure. The weather is at its best, and the visiting and potlatching continue. In the old days, this was the time for war parties to go forth in search of slaves, or to revenge some past injury. When trading posts were established at Victoria, in British Columbia, and in Puget Sound, Washington, the Tlingit often made this voyage of some nine hundred miles, feasting with friendly tribes and fighting their way through enemy country.

Eskudiši (August). During June and July, there is very little storage of food—what is collected is eaten. But in August, storage activities begin again. Women go out for berries, sometimes staying several days. The berries are put into large food boxes, and eulachon oil is poured over them; when tightly covered they will keep fresh for a long time. The Indians have fresh berries in the middle of winter by storing them in this manner. Salmon eggs are also mixed with the berries and the oil and stored away for winter use.

Any meat that is to be stored is hunted and dried in this month. In the old days, deer would be surrounded by men and dogs and driven into the water where they were easily killed by men in canoes. Hunting mountain goats was more difficult. They had to be driven over cliffs or into narrow gorges where men and dogs were able to kill them. The hunters always ate the fat from the viscera immediately after the kill. The meat was cut into long strips and dried in the sun. It would also be broiled in large pieces and put away in eulachon oil. Black bear was also killed by means of deadfalls and the meat both dried and eaten fresh.

Nuškeah (September). This month is perhaps of the greatest economic importance to the Tlingit. He now has to catch and dry his staple food, the salmon. When the village is not on a large river, the people have to go to their clan salmon streams. Here they have temporary shelter and large racks for drying the fish. This is a time of great activity. The men go out each morning to their favorite pools where the salmon have gathered at night. If the water is deep the barbed spear or harpoon is used, if shallow the fish can be driven near the bank where they can be clubbed and picked up by hand. By this time the salmon are getting thinner and weaker and are more easily caught. The tail of the female fish is worn from digging a depression in the river bottom to deposit her eggs. The male fish develops a beak with large teeth in order to hold on to sticks and stones while depositing his sperm over the eggs. The fish get red and black in color; their eyes and fins decay bit by bit until there is little left but the torso. Finally, the half-dead fish become stranded on the banks where they are eaten by crows, gulls, and bears.

When the salmon are brought into camp, the women remove

their heads and entrails, split them, and hang them on the racks, flesh side out. After a week or two rows upon rows of red fish are seen drying in the sun, keeping the children busy in driving off the gulls, crows, ravens, and magpies that are ever hovering about. While the fish are a poorer quality in September, the weather is now so cold that the flies have disappeared, making drying in the open air possible. Smoke houses are also used, the fish being cured by cold smoke.

By the end of September the boxes and baskets are full of dried salmon, and the Indian returns to his winter village. It is a pleasant sight to see the fish-laden canoes drifting down the streams and inlets in the hazy autumn weather, the Indians chanting as they paddle homeward to the feast and the potlatch. The harvest has been gathered and for another year the village will be secure from famine.

Takuna (October). Hunting for direct consumption is the chief occupation. The deer and mountain goat are now at their best, and the snow has not yet become too deep on the mountainsides. Short trading expeditions are made into the interior while the passes are still open. Young men are sent out by the chiefs on extended trips inviting people to come to the potlatch. There is plenty and the heart of the Indian is glad. Now he can plan to further his social position by elaborate feasts and gifts.

Kišina (November). This month is the time of ceremonials. The men do no work while the women attend only to their household duties. As the feast and the potlatch will be described later we shall not go into them here. The days are short and the long rainy nights are conducive to feasting and story telling.

Tleduša (December). Ceremonial activities continue in this month, but some attention is also paid to the preparation of bark and roots for basket making, wool for weaving, and porcupine quills for decoration. In the old days, men prepared wood, stone, and shell for tool making. They went into the forest to find good trees for canoe making and for house timbers. On the islands December is very wet; on the mainland snow begins to fall heavily.

Dagaduša (January). Only a few ceremonials are given, for most of the time is put into manufacturing. In the past, women busied themselves in making garments out of skins and furs. Now they give most of their time to weaving and basket making. If there are totem poles and canoes to be made, the men go off into the woods to do the rough work. When the canoe or the pole has its main outlines, it is dragged to the village where it is finished, accompanied by the expert advice of everyone. When the weather is bad, the men make ceremonial articles, such as masks and rattles and tools for everyday use.

Neškaduša (February). Men begin to prepare for deep sea fishing. They overhaul their hooks and lines, get better sinkers and new bladders for floats. Everyone is watching for signs of good weather, for the stored food has become unpalatable. The most energetic of the young men go out for short fishing trips on the fine days. Ceremonialism has ceased and the people are waiting to begin a new cycle of economic activities.

An analysis of the cycle of production reveals, first of all, a relationship between the various kinds of food collecting activities. In March, deep sea fishing and trout fishing begin and are the chief source of food supply. But the amount of time devoted to them diminishes in April, when time is needed for the collection of seaweed and shellfish and also for the hunting of grouse and other small game. In May, fishing again becomes important, for in this month the oil-producing fish are caught. In this period, fishing is very intense and almost all other activities cease for about two weeks while the people go to their various fishing grounds to catch the oil fish and reduce them to oil. Herbs, roots, and bark are also gathered in May, and much of it is put away for winter use.

These spring activities are governed largely by the seasonal appearance of the various food species, but quality also plays a part. Deep sea fishing and shellfish gathering can be carried on during most of the year but, in the spring, the quality of the cod, halibut, herring, and shellfish is at its best, which partly accounts for their storage at this period.

In June and July, food gathering activities are devoted to immediate consumption only. During these months time is quite evenly distributed between deep sea fishing, hunting, herb and root collecting, and the picking of early berries.

From March until July, deep sea fishing and trout fishing form the major portion of the food collecting activities, followed by the collecting of such shore foods as shellfish and seaweeds. Hunting for furs, in March and April, and for small game throughout this period takes a relatively small part of the natives' time. In July and August, deep sea fishing practically ceases altogether for the salmon now crowd the streams and the Indians leave their winter villages and journey to their clan salmonberry and cranberry patches that grow on the banks of the salmon streams. Thus, as deep sea fishing ceases, salmon fishing takes its place as the major food collecting activity.

In September, the weather is cool and dry, the flies have disappeared, and the rivers are low so that salmon catching is easy. Nearly all time and energy are now devoted to the catching of salmon; by way of variety a few black bears and deer are hunted.

October sees the end of the food collecting activities. Hunters go out for deer, mountain goat, and small game, the meat of which is dried and smoked. In October, the Indians return to the winter villages.

Figure 2 shows the relative amounts of time devoted to the various food getting activities in each month and also the totals for the entire food collecting period which extends from March to the end of October. From this diagram it is easily seen that fishing is the most important food getting activity of the Tlingit.

We shall now examine the storage activities which, on the whole, tend to follow the collecting activities. In March and April, when sea fish, shellfish, and seaweeds are gathered, they are also dried and stored away. In May, oil making forms the chief activity with some attention paid to the preparation and drying of herbs and roots.

In June and July, storage activities cease except in those regions where seal oil is prepared. In August, the storage curve begins to rise as berries are preserved in oil or pressed into cakes and dried. Salmon drying and smoking takes up most of the month of September. October is the month when meat is dried, smoked, and stored. Figure 3 illustrates the storing activities.

Manufacturing, which is the winter activity, commences in November and becomes more intense until it reaches its peak in January, after which it falls away in February to give way to deep sea fishing in March. It is necessary here to point out only the rough outlines of these activities. In November, the women prepare the cedar bark, spruce roots, porcupine quills, mountain goat's wool, sinews, furs, and hides which are to be used for making clothing, baskets, blankets, and mats. The men go out

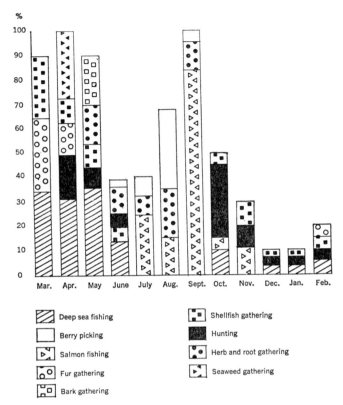

Figure 2. The relative amounts of time spent each month on the gathering
of resources

and bring in what wood they need for their handicrafts or select trees in the forest for the making of canoes, totem poles, or house timbers. In December, January, and February, the women make their blankets, baskets, mats, and clothing, while the men are busy making boxes for food, tools, weapons, ceremonial articles, canoes, and totem poles.

Trading is here considered only as a time-consuming activity carried on for the purpose of barter. Gift exchanges within the village will be ignored here. From this point of view trading becomes a specialized activity carried on from the last week in May until early in July and forms an important part of the entire activity of this period.

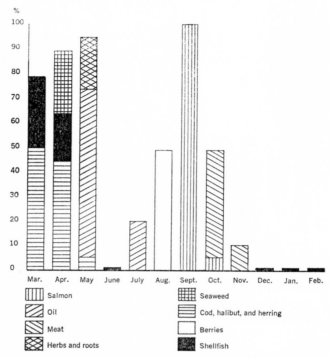

Figure 3. The relative amounts of time spent each month on the storage
activities

The fundamental economic activities have now been outlined,
and their cyclical nature and relative importance are represented
in Figure 4. But the relationship between these so-called economic
activities and the entire social activity still remains to be indicated.
Collective and individual activities, other than those carried on
for economic purposes, are here classed as ceremonial. Among
these ceremonial activities we must class house building and other
forms of ceremonial labor which will be discussed later. It will
suffice here to show the time-consuming relationship between the
fundamental economic activities—collecting, storing, manufacturing, trading—and ceremonialism.

During March, April, and May, when preserved foods have
been exhausted and the energy of the Indian is devoted to not
only the gathering of salt water foods but to their storage, the

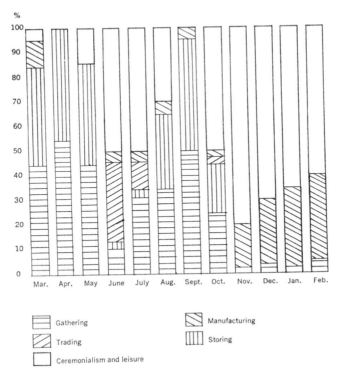

Figure 4. The relative amounts of time spent each month on the important activities

Gathering   Manufacturing

Trading   Storing

Ceremonialism and leisure

winter ceremonialism draws to a close. There exists at all times, of course, those necessary ceremonies incident to marriage, birth, death, sickness, and the settlement of disputes. June and the first half of July are devoted largely to ceremonialism and trading. Storage activities cease and food for direct consumption is easily obtained. This is a period for the great potlatches, as traveling from one village to another is pleasant and safe. This also is the period for house building and the erection of totem poles.

Toward the end of July and in August the Indians leave their permanent villages for their salmon streams. Berry picking and storage form the chief activities of August while September is given entirely to salmon fishing and storage. Ceremonialism is here at a minimum. In October meat storing and the moving of the accumulated dried salmon and meat back to the winter village take up most of the time.

November is pre-eminently a month of feasting, dancing, and potlatching. The storage houses are full and the rainy weather and long nights are conducive to indoor activities. In December manufacturing is taken up in earnest, and ceremonialism becomes less important. But taken as a whole the winter period is intermittently punctuated by social gatherings which consume much time and many food supplies.

War does not form an institutionalized activity among the Tlingit. There is no warrior class and war is not an accredited means to wealth and renown. The slaves owned by the Tlingit were in a large part bartered from the Tsimshian and Haida. Feuds occurred occasionally between the Tlingit clans, but the fighting was seldom of great social importance. Organized fighting did not fit into the general scheme of activities, and when it did occur it upset the even progress of economic and social life. This state of affairs is in sharp contrast to the raiding activities which were carried on by the Plains Indians and which formed an important part of their culture. The accompanying figures endeavor to show the relative importance of the main classes of activities carried on by the Tlingit during the year. The results arrived at were not statistically obtained but are rough approximations based on conversations with old men of several Tlingit villages.

V

THE ORGANIZATION OF LABOR

So far we have observed how production is affected by technology, such social conceptions as exist of magic and art, and finally how production conforms to seasonal changes. It now remains to be shown how social structure and religious beliefs give production its special form.

We can begin by saying that the basic production unit is the house-group, for it is by this group that the important food collecting and storing activities are carried on. In the morning, some male member of the house lights a fire, after which the women of the house prepare the morning meal collectively over the single fire burning in the middle of the room. Keeping the house supplied with firewood is a constant task which is performed collectively by the young men of the house, and which used to be delegated to slaves if the house was fortunate enough to possess some. Wood is not stored. Every other day or so men can be seen going into the forest for dry branches and trunks of dead trees. Even in winter, when deep snow makes wood gathering difficult, there is no effort made on fine days to store wood for stormy days. The wood they gather is generally cottonwood or cedar, the poorest firewood available, but, on the other hand, the most easily obtained.

The great fishing activities of early spring, when men go out for days in search of cod, halibut, and herring, are collective activities, as are the eulachon oil making of May and the salmon fishing of September. Hunting in the autumn formerly was also a collective activity which sometimes stepped out of the bounds of the house-group. The entire clan of a village went to its sealing islands and worked together in the reduction of oil. In hunting mountain goat today, a number of house-groups often work together, and even the brothers of the men's wives, although they are of a different phratry, are invited to come along and to share in the proceeds of the hunt. This is especially true of houses, which, as mentioned before, are closely linked by ties of marriage, blood, and rank. The making of large canoes used in trading is also an activity carried on collectively by men of a house-group.

The digging of shellfish and the collection of berries, roots, and herbs is the collective work of the women of the house-group. If the source of supply is near the village, the women go alone but if it is distant the men go along to protect the women from wild animals. The men, however, are loath to pick berries or gather herbs—to do, in fact, anything which is considered women's work—and they generally loaf about until the women are ready to go home.

Thus the fundamental food collecting activities are collectively performed by members of the house-group. This maintains the economic security of the household. But this does not imply that an individual cannot go hunting or fishing by himself. At any time, when he is not engaged in a collective activity, a man can go into the forest for small game or out to sea for fresh fish and can use his catch himself. This rule demands that the larders must be full of stored food before a man is free to do as he pleases, but the rule is not always strictly adhered to, although, generally speaking, the needs of the household come before the private needs of the individual.

The handicrafts, on the other hand, are individual pursuits. Men make tools, utensils, and weapons for their own use or for the purpose of exchange. Women make blankets, robes, baskets, and clothing for the use of their immediate families or for trade. Services, like those of the carver, shaman, and song maker, are paid for, and the individual specialist has the rights to his reward. We shall put off until Chapter VI how the proceeds of individual effort are dealt with by the house-group, for, while it is true that the individual is the owner of the product of his labor, custom demands that certain apportionments have to be made if he is to maintain his social position.

The clan is not a producing unit, its function being political and ceremonial. The phratry, on the other hand, has economic functions which, on the productive side, may be termed ceremonial labor. This ceremonial labor is not collective labor in the sense that we have applied the term to the labor of the house-group. In the house-group the resources are common property, and the products of labor are shared by the members of the house-group according to individual needs. And, furthermore, the members of a house-group, with the exception of the *yitsati* ("keeper of the house"), all participate in producing activities. Phratral labor, however, is performed by certain relatives on the opposite side. As this labor is ceremonial, not only the members of one of the paired houses but all the opposites of the village are present and take part in the work. Phratral or ceremonial labor is performed theoretically by one's brothers-in-law. For this labor the workers are rewarded by public payments, and all those present are feasted and given small gifts.

Phratral labor consists of such tasks as house building and burial on the collective side, and lip, ear, and nose piercing and totem pole carving on the individual side. These tasks are obligatory and ritualistic. The Tlingit house, as stated before, is sacred, burial is a religious performance, and so are the acts by which a youth is prepared for adult life. An example or two of such joint tasks as house building and burial will be given to show how those activities are carried out.

The seventh Frog house of the Ganaxtedi clan of Klukwan was built in 1908; therefore, modern equipment was used but the underlying pattern was still predominantly Tlingit. When the old house threatened to become uninhabitable, the old men of the house began to talk about building a new one. The matter was later fully discussed, not only by the people of the Frog house but by the whole clan division of the village. When it was finally agreed that the resources of the Frog house people were sufficient to warrant a new house, the *yitsati* came out through the ceremonial opening in the screen before the back wall and announced to the gathered clansmen that a new house was to be built. Next the Wolf people, or members of the opposite phratry, were informed to hold themselves in readiness for the coming task. The Frog house people then began to accumulate food supplies; more salmon, eulachon oil, and berries were stored than usual; blankets and money were accumulated by trade so that a year later the Wolf people began work.

The Wolf people selected for the task were members of the village and were, generally, the sons of the men of the Frog house and the brothers of the wives of the Frog house men. Any Wolf man was liable for the task but close relatives were first called upon. In the old days, the Wolf men went into the woods, cut and prepared the timbers, and allowed them to season. In modern times, the Raven people bought the necessary lumber and nails, but the Wolf people brought them up the Chilcat River in canoes, a distance of twenty-two miles. During the actual construction the *yitsati* of the Frog house supervised the work while his kinsmen prepared food for the workers. Wolf men of high status worked on the building along with men of lesser status, but they abstained from the heavier tasks. Other Wolves not occupied on the building came around giving advice and watched the progress of the work. In the old days, when the corner post holes were sunk, slaves were killed and their bodies placed beneath the posts. During the work, the Frog house people provided the builders with the best possible foods and entertained them with jokes and songs. The whole activity was an occasion for jollity and merrymaking. The completion of the house was, of course, an occasion for a great potlatch in which the actual builders were publicly rewarded.

Another instance of ceremonial labor performed jointly by members of one phratry for their opposites was the burial of Yehlgak, the *ankaua* (rich man") of the Ganaxtedi, a Raven clan. The day following his death, the women of the Wolf phratry washed the body and laid it out in state. All the emblems of the clan were placed about him along with the modern framed photographs of himself and other deceased Raven chiefs. Next, messengers were sent out to the trapping grounds to bring in all the Wolves and Ravens. In former days, the body would have been cremated, but in 1931 it was placed in a coffin and buried in a Christian manner. The Raven men were very careful not to touch the body while it was being placed in the coffin. While the Wolf people were busy about the body, the Raven people were busy getting food ready for a feast to which the entire village was invited. After the feast, humorous stories were told and everyone seemed happy, for the dead chief was looking on and was glad that such good care had been taken of his body. All the important Raven men remained around the body all night speaking of his deeds and the good things he had done for the villagers. Theoretically the entire village should have remained awake. Paid Wolf women wailed over the body at intervals during the night. The following day the grave was dug by the Wolf men, who then carried the coffin to the grave and lowered it in. Leading Raven men threw a few shovelsful of earth on the coffin after which the Wolf men finished the task.

A year or so after the burial the Raven people bought a gravestone, and the Wolf people were again called into service to erect it. In former days, the Ravens had one of the Wolf men carve a totem pole in which the ashes of the dead were placed, but after the advent of Christian burials the pole was erected over the grave; now, of course, the Indians are beginning to use tombstones. After this event, a potlatch was given in which all those who had worked on the burial, that is, had buried the body and erected the totem pole or tombstone, were rewarded.

While house building and burial are performed by a group of people belonging to the opposite phratry—in cases where the village is small, by the entire opposite side—there are, on the other hand, many activities of a ceremonial nature performed by individuals. When a girl reaches the age of puberty, *wetadi*, and goes into seclusion in preparation for the puberty ceremony, her lower lip is pierced and a bit of bone or wire thrust in the hole. At short intervals larger bits of bone are inserted until the opening will take a plug-shaped labrette. By middle age the opening is large enough to take an elaborately shaped, elongated labrette. The piercing of the lip and the changing of the labrettes is always performed by a near female relative of the opposite side, generally the father's sister or, after marriage, a sister-in-law.

During the period of seclusion, the girl's ear lobes and often the septum of the nose are also pierced. These services, likewise, are performed by the same female relative. In the case of boys, the septum of the nose is pierced and various parts of the body are tattooed. This work is done by the boy's father's brother, a man belonging to the opposite phratry. If these specified relatives do not exist, then some other individual of the opposite side will do, but care must be taken to see that this individual is of the same rank as the boy or girl.

At childbirth the expectant mother retreats to a nearby hut, *yanauskahiti*, which is built anew for each birth. She is attended by her husband's sisters. They cut the umbilical cord with a stone or mussel shell arrow point and put small arrows in the child's cradle for good luck. If the birth appears difficult, a shaman is called who performs a ceremony near the woman invoking the aid of the spirits. Both the attending women and the shaman are paid for their services either immediately or at the time when the child's uncle comes to give it a name.

Another type of ceremonial labor performed by an individual is that of carving totem poles or of carving the totem on a hat, corner post, or any other object. One always selected a man opposite to himself of equal rank, a wife's brother if possible. It sometimes happened that this man was an indifferent carver in which case he was at liberty to hire an expert carver of either phratry to do the work for him. He might even hire a slave. He, however, paid the person that carved the article, and then his brother-in-law paid him in the form of a gift. Tsimshian carvers were noted for their workmanship, and many a Tlingit chief had his house posts carved by one of them at high cost. The man assigned the ceremonial task would himself select the wood, bring it to the village, make a model, and then direct the expert carver. The totem or emblem designs were sacred, and only people of high status could be concerned with them. The payment was thus made to the agent who gave what he thought fit to the actual carver. As emblem carving became more and more important with the introduction of iron and steel tools, the carver also became more and more specialized and important, so the bulk of the payment went to the actual carver but still through the hands of the intermediary.

The above-mentioned types of work may be said to comprise those activities here classed as ceremonial labor. Work of the specialist or professional will be taken up next. The carver, we saw, often performed ceremonial labor, but many kinds of carving were not considered ceremonial. Thus a man might become an expert canoe maker, and others would find it better to pay him for his work than to attempt canoe making for themselves.

Horn spoon carving and tool and weapon making also tended to become the specialized activities of the carver.

Song making also existed as a profession. Song makers, in fact, organized a society in some villages, the purpose of which was to be sure that a plentiful supply of songs were on hand for marriages and deaths, feasts and ridicule. Anyone could go to the society and buy a song or, if he was not satisfied with what was on hand, he could have one made to order, sad or happy, just as he wished.

The shaman (*ixt*) is perhaps the most important specialist among the Tlingit. His services are required in almost every important undertaking, such as war, curing the sick, hunting, fishing, love, and combating witchcraft. In the majority of cases the shaman is required to reveal the future so that human activities can be governed accordingly. On war parties, in former days, the Tlingit always carried their shaman with them in their war canoes. He lay in the center of the canoe covered with a mat and directed the activities of his clansmen. Conflicts were often carried on entirely by shamans who made their respective spirits bring about supernatural happenings, such as lights at night, new headlands in the inlets, or other miracles.

Shamans held a high position and demanded high rewards which made them very much the allies of the wealthy. Today, Tlingit shamans inherit their positions and their spirits from their uncles and go through an elaborate initiatory training period.

Labor is also organized along the lines of sex, age, and status. Some activities are strictly limited to either men or women, while others, again, can be jointly carried on. Among the male activities are house building; canoe making; carving of all kinds; tool, weapon, and utensil making; trading; hunting and fishing. Women carry on such activities as preparing meals and cleaning the house; cleaning, drying, and storing fish; making clothing; preparing hides and furs; weaving baskets, mats, and blankets; gathering and storing seaweed, shellfish, roots, herbs, and berries. While women weave the sacred clan emblems into blankets and baskets, they are not supposed to understand these emblems. Thus the men always make the patterns on wooden boards from which the women copy the designs. If a man is caught doing women's work, he is laughed at. Likewise, women are always careful to perform only those tasks which belong to them. There are also certain activities which are jointly carried on by men and women, such as oil making, bark gathering, berry picking, and the making of ceremonial articles and decorations.

Child care falls as much upon the men as upon the women. When boys come to their mother's brother's house, the uncle spends a great deal of time training them. He takes them out every morning, winter or summer, and forces them to bathe in the sea or the river. He teaches them the songs and stories of their clan, shows them the clan hunting and fishing grounds, and in every way prepares them to carry on the traditions of their people. The daughters who stay at home with their mother and father are also carefully trained, especially during the time of seclusion and puberty. In the old days, this period often lasted as long as a year. While they are kept away from social contacts, they are taught proper behavior, how to weave, and how to take care of children. Both the father and the mother make every effort to prepare the girl for a successful marriage, for, while the girl's status is of the utmost importance, her appearance, character, and manners are never lost sight of.

While traveling, women paddle with the men if extra paddlers are necessary. Women carry burden baskets on their backs, held in place by a tump line. Women often accompany trading expeditions—the Indians saying that women are better bargainers than men. Women are often seen carrying heavy loads while men saunter along emptyhanded. This is owing, not to the laziness of the husband nor to his cruelty, but to the contents of the basket. A Tlingit would no more think of carrying a basketful of berries, roots, or herbs than would many a white man of doing his wife's Monday morning washing.

Age has, on the whole, very little to do with labor, although in the house-group certain activities are performed by the uncles, while others are performed by the nephews. These activities, however, correlate as much with physical ability as with age. In hunting or fishing the older men do the directing, while the younger do the heavy work, such as driving deer into the water, or mountain goats into the narrow defiles or ravines in the mountains. During potlatches the nephews wait on the guests while the uncles act as hosts.

Status, on the other hand, is of great importance in the organization of labor. While the *yitsati* initiates all important activities, he tends to abstain from the more strenuous forms of common labor. He never gathers wood nor carries water, nor is he ever seen preparing food. As his position is primarily ceremonial, he is careful not to endanger his prestige nor that of his house by doing menial tasks. His chief economic function is to decide when it is best to go hunting, or to begin the salmon harvest, or to go to prepare oil. This he does by watching the position of the sun. When it has passed certain landmarks, then it is time to undertake the various economic activities. The *yitsati* is also the judge of quality in foods, especially oils. In the old days, each house tried to make the best oil, and each *yitsati* had his special formula for oil making, which consisted largely in letting the fish decay for a certain length of time before rendering the oil.

The *yitsati* was the trader in the old trading days. He saw to it that certain goods were accumulated for trading purposes. His brothers and nephews could accumulate private wealth which they traded individually, but the primary object of the trading expedition was the acquisition of articles required by the housegroup which it did not produce at all, or not so well. On trading trips the *yitsati* sat in the middle of the canoe (the place of honor) while one of his brothers or the ablest nephew did the navigating. If an expedition over land took place, the *yitsati* never carried anything but his weapons and personal articles.

If the *yitsati* belongs to the *anyeti* ("noble class"), he is even more divorced from common labor. This, of course, applies to all members of the *anyeti* whether they are house chiefs or not. A high-born Tlingit does little outside ceremonial activities other than amuse himself. He will scarcely speak to anyone but his equal. Common labor is quite impossible if he wishes to maintain his prestige. *Anyeti* women are not taught the common art of weaving but cultivate only mannerisms of speech and movement. In fact girls who have never worked are considered special prizes to be won in marriage.

The property aspects of slavery have already been discussed in connection with the general forms of property. Here it will be necessary to describe slavery from the point of view of labor power. We have seen that, economically speaking, labor can be divided into common and ceremonial. Slaves were not permitted to carry on ceremonial tasks. Exceptions to this rule were made in instances where a slave possessed great talent, as in carving.

He might then be permitted to perform a ceremonial task, but even here the task was nominally performed by a man of recognized rank, and the slave's position was much like that of a tool.

Slaves' work, formerly, consisted of the menial tasks of collecting firewood, fetching water, cleaning fish and game, and generally taking care of the household duties. Food preparation and service on ceremonial occasions, however, were delegated to the young men and women of the house-group. As has already been mentioned, food and the food animals and plants were not sacred among the Tlingit so that slaves could participate in all the major food collecting activities such as hunting, fishing, and plant gathering. Slaves, likewise, participated in all the handicrafts, except the making of ceremonial objects, which they were only allowed to do under supervision when they possessed great talent. While the Tlingit possessed slaves, it would be erroneous to think of Tlingit economy as a slave economy, using this term to imply that the slaves were exploited solely for their labor power. The Tlingit slave was a piece of property, an instrument for certain social purposes, which were more important than the use of a slave as a means for producing material wealth or providing services. These social purposes will be treated in connection with the study of the potlatch in Chapter VIII.

The study of the organization of labor would not be complete without a discussion of the standards of work. One of the surprising things that strikes an observer is the fact that the Tlingit have more time than they need. The utilization of time in economic and ceremonial activities does not exhaust all their waking hours. To a person working in an industrial society, where one time-task has to be balanced against another, time is of the utmost value, and it is difficult to realize that there is time which is not actively spent and yet not felt to be wasted. The Tlingit have a habit of sitting around, singly or in groups, for half a day at a time with scarcely a word being uttered by anyone. Furthermore, no matter how early in the morning or how late at night one goes to an Indian village, there are always men sauntering about with apparently no purpose in mind. Before sunrise is a favorite time, especially for old men, to wander out of the village along the beach or on the hillsides. They have neither arms nor tools and, if asked what they are doing, they reply to the effect that they are just looking around. This idle sitting or aimless walking, as it appears to a white man, may have some deeper psychological meaning to the Indian, but the writer could find no social justification for it other than that the Indian did not know what to do with his surplus time. The dates for the beginning and ending of the great food gathering activities are set by seasonal changes which custom has formalized into a calendar. Between the dates set for a task, the Tlingit works, as it seems to us, very leisurely. Men go to work after a light morning meal and remain until about three or four o'clock in the afternoon when they return and eat a large meal. They never return to work after this meal, unless unforeseen circumstances force them to do so. Six or seven hours seem to be the average working day. There is no specific time of day for beginning work, as so much depends upon the weather, the tides, and the movements of fish and animals.

The intensity with which the Tlingit work is also much less than that of their white neighbors. In using the seine and the gill-net, the Indians take frequent rest periods and while in action move more slowly than white men. The handling of the same nets is performed by white men with no rest periods. While traveling in canoes, the Tlingit paddle steadily for half an hour and then rest and occasionally every other stroke is interrupted by someone engaging in conversation. To a white man all of the Indian's economic actions are slowly performed. Also, a Tlingit never feels that he must have a task finished by a certain time, which makes it difficult to hurry him on. This lack of speed is not owing to physical weakness, for during ceremonials the same men will go through long dances demanding the greatest agility and speed. In athletics the Tlingit are a match for their untrained white neighbors. The intensity with which a Tlingit works, therefore, is due to a standard set by his society.

The efficiency of a Tlingit workman is, likewise, a matter settled by the standards set by his society's needs. In the use and care of his gun he seems to be very careless, yet in carving a lid for a food box his skill is remarkable. The results of Tlingit handicraft show patience, ingenuity, and ability of a high order. Teachers in the mission schools claim that Tlingit children consistently show lower averages in intelligence tests than do white children—mixed bloods being intermediate. The results might have been different if the tests had been made up of questions bearing on how to recognize various birds from their flight, the habits of animals, or how far a child could trace back his ancestry, or again, how well he knew the mythology of his society. A Tlingit, like everyone else, is efficient where his society demands that he be efficient.

VI

THE DISTRIBUTION OF WEALTH

Distribution is that aspect of economic behavior which deals with the customs and institutions, rules and regulations by which goods and services are transferred from the point of production to the point of consumption. This transfer, however, is not primarily the movement of goods and services, although that is implied, but is a matter, fundamentally, of the transfer of ownership. Every culture defines the mechanisms by which the transfer of ownership is made and the forces which determine the amounts involved in these transfers. In Tlingit economy the mechanisms of distribution are of three general types: (1) those connected with the sharing of the collectively produced product, (2) the institutions of exchange, and (3) the system of economic rights or privileges.

The sharing of the collectively produced product takes place almost entirely within the house-group. The staple foods and the fuel are collectively produced, and we find that they are consumed in common. In this situation, however, to discover the mechanisms of apportionment we must determine the manner in which the commodities are utilized. The house is heated by a large central fire, and thus the problem of sharing the fuel does not arise. In the case of the staple foods, however, the matter is somewhat different. Meals are cooked and eaten around a central fire, each person taking his or her share out of a large cooking pot. We see, therefore, that the mechanism of apportionment of the staple foods is identical with the mechanism of their consumption within the house-group. But this type of consumption and apportionment must be clearly distinguished from that taking place at a feast to which outsiders are invited.

Yet all foods in the house-group are not communally produced and consumed. As has already been pointed out in Chapter III, individuals could go out hunting or fishing and keep the proceeds themselves. This private consumption of food applies generally to such rare articles of diet as grouse and ptarmigan, big horn sheep and black cod. These scarce foods are cooked and eaten at the central fire by a man and his family, and the other members of the group do not feel any resentment as they are at liberty to go out and procure these things for themselves. But should there happen to be more than the hunter and his family can consume at one meal, it is indiscriminately handed out to the other members of the house-group.

The principle which determines the amount of the shares of food is individual want. Barring a time of shortage each person satisfies his need for food. On the whole, everyone eats the same foods, although it is said that great chiefs ate by themselves and took the best portions of fish and game. On ceremonial occasions this is certainly true, but in ordinary life chiefs and elders in general could make this demand, not because of a fixed rule but through the prerogative of age. One way of showing respect for the older men was by giving them the best foods.

In the case of the *yitsati* ("keeper of the house"), a formalized way of showing respect was through a food gift given to him by the young men of the house. We have already spoken of the individual hunting and fishing, and even today it is always the custom for a hunter or a fisherman to give the house chief a portion of his bag or catch. The question of amount is left entirely to the giver. The economic function of this food gift is to provide the *yitsati* with luxury foods which he cannot procure for himself owing to the fact that he is a ceremonial leader and not a hunter or fisherman. The *yitsati*, in turn, rewards the giver by taking a personal interest in his private affairs. Furthermore, there is the factor of the *yitsati*'s social position in the house-group which is kept before the minds of the others by these formal gifts of food.

The above description shows that the primary needs for food and shelter are satisfied communally within the confines of the house-group. Sharing is done through consuming based upon the principle of individual need. In cases where scarce goods are collectively produced, such as bear skins, seal skins, or the proceeds of a trading expedition, the *yitsati* takes a hand in their distribution among the members of the house-group. The principle, here again, is one of individual need. We can see from this that the house-group is economically closely integrated, even more so than the individual family. A man and wife are dependent economic units within the larger and more stable economic group.

By the term exchange, the second category of mechanisms for the distribution of wealth, we can differentiate that large field of economic behavior, the function of which is to link up the interdependent units of production and consumption, which in turn have arisen through the territorial distribution of natural resources and the specialization of technological processes. Exchange, therefore, comprises all those customs and institutions which transfer the ownership of goods and services from one individual and group to another. Among the Tlingit these institutions and mechanisms of exchange are clearly defined. Every Tlingit makes distinctions between such institutions as barter, gift exchange, the food gift, the feast, the ceremonial exchange of labor, and the ceremonial gift. But while these institutions of exchange are concerned with material goods and services, while, in other words, they are economic, their sociological aspects are so important that to treat them solely as the mechanisms for the transfer of utilities would be to miss their full social significance. We must, therefore, indicate the direct needs which every specific transaction of exchange fulfills, both for the individuals concerned and for the group as a whole. There is an essential difference in function between barter and the ceremonial gift, and logical consistency would demand that we begin with pure barter and run through the less complex institutions to the most complex one, namely, the potlatch. But trade involves so many factors that it will be left until the next chapter to be treated fully. All that need be pointed out here is that trade, *wutsisex*, tends to be the most purely economic of the exchange transactions and as such was not formerly practiced by the Tlingit among themselves. The act of pure barter fulfills one direct need, namely, the acquisition of the object. The individuals involved seek their own advantage through bargaining and tend to ignore the system of relationships which makes them members of a community. To a Tlingit barter and bargaining are incompatible with his social relationships and attitudes, and he has, therefore, developed exchange mechanisms which not only take cognizance of these relationships but are instrumental in shifting or maintaining them. We shall, then, begin with the gift exchange, *lauxu.*

Articles of clothing, tools, weapons, and ceremonial objects are individually produced and are used by the maker or are exchanged by him for other articles, which he is not so proficient in making. This exchange of individually produced articles, among the Tlingit themselves, always takes the form of a gift, *lauxu.* The same is true of a reward given for services. This rule holds even within the house-group where so much is produced and held in common.

If a man wants someone to make him an object, he gives that person a preliminary gift and makes his wish known. He will not ask the man outright but will admire the object he desires in the possession of the craftsman, or he will use an intermediary who will take the preliminary gift to the craftsman and make his wishes known. The social norm demands that a man accept a gift and also that he return one. On the economic level no difficulty is caused by this formalized gift method of payment. The value of objects are very well known, so that if one wishes an object of quality he is forced to give the maker a gift of the proper value in return. The craftsman can always retaliate upon a stingy giver by making a poor article.

If the article is of small value, for example, a bone harpoon or a cooking box, the first gift will be sufficient to reward the craftsman. More expensive articles, such as canoes, ceremonial robes, and shell ornaments are paid for by two and sometimes three presentations of gifts. The ceremonial articles here referred to are not to be confused with the crests and emblems. Ceremonial objects like masks, robes, and rattles are not considered sacred and can be made by anyone. Furthermore, these exchanges can be carried on between women as well as between men. Especially within the village, women specialize in basketry and fur and hide work and exchange these articles among themselves.

The song makers and speakers are paid by a gift given during the occasion for which they have composed the song or given the speech. Besides the regular songs, anyone of the guests can get up and sing a song in honor of the host's nephew or daughter, for which the host must immediately give a gift. The gift must be a considerable one, if the host wishes to keep his social position unimpaired.

The shaman, on the other hand, is paid in a very formal way. When a man wishes the services of a shaman he collects a quantity of furs, robes, and articles of food and piles them on the floor of his house. He then sends a messenger for the shaman. The shaman comes and looks at the gifts, and if he is satisfied he will go home and send a return messenger saying that he will proceed with the task, whatever it may be, but that he will require such-and-such an amount at its completion. The man desiring the shaman has then to signify his agreement and to make his home ready for a shamanistic performance either by removing the totemic crests or by covering them with robes. The payment of the shaman seems to be contrary to the gift nature of exchange for the element of bargaining enters. This, however, is in conformity with the general position of the shaman in Tlingit society. He is, as has been stated in the chapter on social organization, not so intimately a part of the social group as the other people. He lives much of his time apart from his relatives and is buried outside the village.

At the birth of a child the expectant mother is attended by her husband's sister who is rewarded for her services by a presentation of gifts. The child's maternal uncle comes to give the child a name when the child is about a year old, and he also is rewarded with a gift for this service. This first name is not of great social importance and cannot be confused with the ancestral names passed on to a young man when he comes of age. These important names are always given at potlatches.

The above-mentioned services are transactions, strictly speaking, between the two parties concerned. While custom determines the value of the service, there is the added factor of rank, which makes even these ostensibly private negotiations public. If a high ranking, wealthy *yitsati* refuses to give a more valuable gift than a *yitsati* of lesser rank for a service of equal value, this fact will become known throughout the village, and the greater chief will be shamed in the eyes of the villagers. Bargaining on the purely economic level tends to be kept out of even the most minor material transaction, and the gift exchange takes into account the status relationship of the individual concerned. Thus when one Tlingit gives another Tlingit a gift of this kind, not only are their economic needs satisfied, but their mutual social positions are publicly expressed. We have already seen how this operates in the house-group where the men are constantly giving small gifts to the *yitsati* in recognition of his position.

Besides these payments and exchanges which take the form of a gift, the Tlingit are constantly giving gifts of food to the different members of the village community. The collectively produced food of the house-group is often shared among the other houses of the same clan. If the men of the house-group are fortunate in getting a large catch of fish or game, they will take what they think they can use and leave the rest on the beach. The other houses of the same clan then send the women of their house-groups to take as much as they can use. If there is still some left over, the original owners parcel it out and take it to their fathers and brothers-in-law who are in the opposite phratry. There is no strict account kept of these food transactions but everyone endeavors to return the gifts. During a food shortage, those lucky enough to have a supply always distribute it among the villagers. For this they are rewarded publicly at some future potlatch and their renown is kept alive through songs and stories.

We now come to the feast, *wuš-kana-wuti-at* (literally, "we gather together"). While potlatches, ceremonials, marriages, and public gatherings of any kind are accompanied by feasts, a man or house-group is also free to give a feast on any private occasion. The most common occasions for feasting are those connected with success in hunting, fishing, and the return of a successful expedition. The house-group will then invite its nearest relatives and great quantities of food will be consumed in common, what is not eaten being carried away by the guests.

When a young man returns from his shamanistic training period, his relatives give a feast in his honor. For months he has been away from the village in some secluded valley with older shamans, who have taught him how to get in touch with his supernatural helpers. He is thin from fasting and the various physical and mental efforts through which he has had to go. If he has been successful, his relatives rejoice and give him a feast in compensation for his trials.

In Chapter VIII the feast will be discussed as an instrument of consumption and we shall then see much more fully the details of its form. The emphasis here is laid chiefly upon the occasions for feasting and the forces which determine its extent. Feasts, among the Tlingit, are almost an everyday occurrence and range from the simple feast in which several households participate to one which lasts for days and in which several villages take part. Every *yitsati* wishes to return all the feasts which he has attended and to regale his visitors to an equal extent, at least. He will, however, if he has the means, endeavor to outdo all the other feasts both in the number of dishes and in the quantity of food.

The feast is primarily a house-group affair. The food for the ordinary feast is accumulated by the members of a house-group and is prepared by the women and served by the young men. The point to keep in mind is that the feast, *wuš-kana-wuti-at*, as such, is not a ritual matter. As has been pointed out, in former days slaves could prepare and serve the food. A man gives a feast because he "feels-good-inside." But if the feast is a part of a burial ceremony, a wedding, or a potlatch, it becomes, like the event with which it is connected, a ritual, and slaves were not permitted to serve or to be present at the eating. It is then, also, a clan affair and members of the clan may be called upon to contribute food.

As a rule, the more important the guest, the more sumptuous the feast. But the pure feast, that is, group eating unconnected with ritual, does not primarily depend upon social obligations to people of rank. As already mentioned, the feast is given when the house has been fortunate in getting a large supply of food. It is only then that a feast is proposed and guests thought of.

It is by now obvious that the feasts and the gift have a number of important economic and social characteristics and functions. Let us look at these institutions, first of all, from the economic standpoint. In discussing the gift and the feast, we have really been talking about three fundamental economic transactions, namely, the exchange of commodities, the payment of services, and the investment of the surplus. In an economy where there is neither market nor an established form of money, the feast and the gift perform these necessary functions without which an economic system could not operate.

The gift, as a mechanism for the exchange of commodities and a mechanism for the payment of services, performs at once an individual and a social function. Through it an individual is permitted the wider satisfaction of his wants. He can command articles which he cannot make himself, and he can specialize in the making of objects for which he is especially fitted and from which he derives an emotional satisfaction. The social benefit arises out of the fact that the ordinary gift, although not a sacred or ceremonial affair, is not a matter for bargaining; bargaining being, as we have seen, disruptive to the social relationships that exist. The ordinary gift, *lauxu*, must be differentiated, on the one hand, from the ceremonial gift, *xu'ix*, and from pure trade, *wutsisex*, on the other. About the exchange of gifts, *lauxu*, therefore, the Tlingit places certain social restrictions which make exchanges, within his own community, take into consideration the social status of the individuals concerned. A Tlingit cannot bargain with another Tlingit but must give him what is his due as a man of social position.

The food gift and the feast have even wider economic ramifications than the gift which is the result of craftsmanship. The food gift and the feast affect both the individual and the group. The men of the house-group are not certain of their luck in always having their house full of the various kinds of food and, as a purely economic matter, it is wise to give gifts to one's relatives so that one will be certain of return gifts in the future. The same applies to the feast. It is really an investment of surplus food in the community at large which will later bring in certain returns to the house that makes the original investment.

Whether the Tlingit is conscious of it or not, the food gift and the feast perform an economic function of the greatest importance to his society. It is easy to see that the food gift and the feast are mechanisms for the distributions of the economic surplus in a productive system where production is still largely dependent upon the risks of the productive units, namely, the house-groups. As mechanisms for the distribution of food, these institutions level the ups and downs in an economy where there is no central market. The food gift and the feast prevent the piling up and wastage of food in certain parts of the community. Furthermore, in times of shortage or famine these institutions are instrumental in enabling the group as a whole to meet these trying situations successfully.

In addition to their purely economic aspects, the gift and the feast also fulfill other needs both of the individual and of the group. From the individual's point of view, the food gift and the feast provide a means for social approval and eminence. While it is true that there is no definite obligation on the part of a man to give these food gifts and feasts, yet the "good man," "the great *ankaua*" ("rich man") is one who has given many feasts to the villagers. Social service is rewarded by social renown and prestige.

The gift and the feast have also functions that affect the solidarity and harmony of the group. We have already seen how the exchange of gifts and services add to the interdependence and thus to the cooperation of individuals. To this must be added the mutual obligations and reciprocal relations arising out of the giving and taking of food gifts and feasts. The feast, especially, coming as it does not at any specified time but whenever the giver has plenty and is, therefore, in a benevolent mood, brings about unity not only physically but emotionally. It is a time of rejoicing and hilarity; a time when serious ceremonies, which often bring antagonisms, are evaded by horseplay and nonsense. If a Tlingit wants to bring a potential enemy to terms, he invites him to a feast. When hunters or fishermen encroached upon the property of another clan, the clansmen could often bring about a settlement by inviting the poachers to a feast after which the visitors would feel ashamed and leave the territory of their hosts in peace.

We come now to a number of institutions that differ considerably from the ordinary exchange of gifts and feasts. In the gift, *lauxu*, and the feast, *wuš-kana-wuti-at*, we saw that, while social motivation and social regulation entered in, the fundamental purpose was economic. It was economic need which caused men to exchange commodities in the form of gifts. It was the economic surplus and the expectation of a return of goods which were fundamental in forcing a man to give a feast to his villagers. But the institution of house building, *hitawutiya*, of bodily decoration, *tukukwatuatak*, and of burial, *yenakututsika*, are much more important socially than the ordinary gift and feast. They are, as has been pointed out in the previous chapter, performed by the members of one phratry to the members of another; they are connected with clans, with the totemic emblems and crests, with the spirits of the ancestors, and with matters of rank.

The first, house building, is fundamentally an economic act

which provides shelter and, viewed from the Tlingit method of production, it is an exchange of services. The Raven people build houses for the Wolf people and the Wolf people, in turn, build houses for the Raven people. Economically speaking, the transaction should end there for, as in the case of the gift exchange, the principle of reciprocity has been substantiated. Yet the whole house-building process is initiated, punctuated, and ended with elaborate feasting and gift giving. The question at once arises, why the gift giving and the feasting? The Tlingit themselves are emphatic in saying that they do not pay the builders, for payment is brought about by return of service.

We could argue that the gift giving here is economic in the same sense as when it is not connected with house building, that is, there is an expectation of gifts, as such, in return, which serve purely economic needs. But when we look at the nature of the gifts, we are at once struck by the fact that they are not consumed in the satisfaction of the needs for food, shelter, and clothing. The very nature of the gifts themselves often debar such usage: in the past they consisted of ceremonial robes, shell ornaments, slaves, and coppers; in recent years they have consisted chiefly of woolen blankets and money. Even goods that could be employed for the satisfaction of economic wants are not used for this purpose but are stored away and used only when the occasion arises for the building of a house, burial, or the preparation of the young for adult life.

In burial and in the preparation of the adolescent for adult life, service cancels service, but here again, gifts are ceremonially handed over to the opposites, who perform the service, during the gathering which terminates these activities.

In analyzing these three ceremonial activities, we observe, from the point of view of exchange, that there are three separate transfers involved, namely, the exchange of labor, the feast, and the exchange of gifts. In the study of social organization and production, we have seen who are the people taking part in ceremonial labor and how they carry on their operations. While the ceremonial exchange of labor is closely connected with kinship, totemism, and rank, there is no doubt that it is fundamentally an economic institution. It is also important to note the sociological function for the exchange of services, for while the linked house-groups are in close contact through marriage and kinship, this relationship is constantly expressed through the mutual exchanges of labor. The feast which always accompanies any large gathering is functionally constant in immediate purpose and social effect, as has already been pointed out. We might also add that the feast, too, is quite definitely an economic institution, however closely related it may be to the particular ceremony of which it is a part.

It is a relatively simple matter to discuss the form, correlations, and purposive content of such institutions as the simple gift, the feast, and the exchange of services, for their economic character and effect upon the culture is quite clear. But once we come to the ceremonial gift, or potlatch as it is more commonly called, we are at once struck by the fact that it is not an economic institution. It is clear that barter, the feast, the gift exchange, and ceremonial labor provide goods and services that are ends in themselves, used for the direct satisfaction of physical needs. In the ceremonial gift or potlatch, however, the central fact is not the acquisition of the gift, nor the use of these goods for economic means. The potlatch is economic to the extent that it uses economic means, that is, there is a transfer of material goods, and the recipient is obliged to return the gift at some future date. The end of the transaction is essentially noneconomic. The social significance of the potlatch is far greater than the social significance of the other exchange mechanisms of Tlingit economy. While the potlatch, like the feast, is a mechanism of distribution, it is at the same time a mechanism of consumption, and it is the consumptive aspect of the potlatch which is of far greater functional importance. We shall therefore treat it fully in the chapter on the consumption of wealth.

Besides house building, burial, and the preparation of the young for adult life, there are two other ritual occasions in which the ceremonial gift plays a leading part, namely, marriage and the settlement of legal disputes. These two ceremonies are never potlatch occasions, nor can we speak of the bride gift and the indemnity as primarily economic acts, for here, as in the potlatch, material wealth is used as a means for the satisfaction of other than economic ends. Hence, we shall treat the bride gift and the indemnity as primarily mechanisms of consumption.

We now have to consider the elements and forces that go to determine the amounts of goods and services that are exchanged. In the house-group we cannot speak of exchange of the staple commodities, such as fish, oil, berries, shelter, large canoes, and fish nets, for they are collectively produced and collectively utilized; individual need is the prime force in apportionment. The *yitsati*, however, has certain economic rights to choice bits of food, for he must abstain from the menial tasks of food gathering.

Such apportionment of goods and services as are made through the feast, food gift, ceremonial labor, and the ceremonial or potlatch gift are also dominated by forces other than those appearing in exchange. That is to say, the study of exchange value does not explain the flow of utilities through those important institutions of distribution in Tlingit economy. In discussing these mechanisms of exchange, it has been pointed out how they correlate with the technological elements of uncertainty in production, the lack of markets, and the social factors of kinship, rank, and individual prestige. This brings us ultimately down to the socially determined standards of work and consumption which set the pattern of Tlingit economy. If we look back at Figure 2, representing the relative amounts of time spent in the acquisition of food, we see both those goods that are of prime importance, like salmon, and those that are less important, such as the flesh of deer and mountain goat. But time alone does not reveal the social importance of the food, for the time devoted to making fish oil is small, but the quantity produced and consumed is very large. Time spent in production and the quantity consumed by the Tlingit as a group determine what is of high social utility and importance. We must here note that the products of high social importance are individually considered very low in exchange value, yet the group as a whole is greatly concerned if something happens to endanger the amount of the supply. The Tlingit saw to it, in former days, that clan salmon rivers were protected against foreign infringement. But the fish supply was secure to the extent that no group rituals were connected with its production or consumption as compared with the ritualism of the Eskimo in sea mammal hunting or the growing of corn among the Indians of the Southwest. Not only were fish and oil of low exchange value among the Tlingit, but the activity of their production was considered common and left to slaves. The principal economic activities among the Tlingit were means and not ends in themselves, which tends to be true where food gathering is not hazardous. The surplus of Tlingit food supply was transformed into potlatch goods and reserves of food which were expended in potlatching, marriage gift, and ceremonialism of all kinds. Economy was thus given increasing importance in the functioning of the culture as opposed to, say, warfare or shamanism. But we must consider economy here always as a means. The great man was not a successful fisherman or hunter as was true of the Eskimo or the Athapascan of northern Canada, but a man who used these goods, not for immediate consumption, but exchanged them for such things as slaves and coppers which were given away at potlatches. He was eminent, not because he was rich in food, but because he had acquired honor through the distribution of goods derived from food.

When we come to the gift exchange and barter, we are in the realm of exchange value where individual forces play a greater part. In assessing the value of any object the Tlingit is dominated by certain considerations that are common to most human beings. The elements going into an evaluation certainly include such considerations as economic utility, esthetic satisfaction, personal associations, display for prestige, and magical or religious efficacy. It is, of course, difficult to separate these elements in a single object, like the Tlingit harpoon, which satisfied at least economic, esthetic, and magical needs, or a crest hat, which served as an index of rank, gave esthetic satisfaction, and had a religious meaning. But it seems that by looking at prime purposes we can say that the harpoon was an economic instrument, and the crest hat served social or religious needs.

All the goods the Tlingit exchanged were valued from these various angles dominated by the underlying forces of scarcity and human effort on the cost side and the intensity of the desire on the demand side. All goods were valued in terms of one another so that the value of any good was made up of the partial values included in its making. The cost of a spear was determined by the values of the green stone, the sinew obtained by barter, and the amount of time put into its manufacture. To this must be added the emotional values of the maker or the prospective purchaser.

Bargaining power was also an important factor in exchange. In the gift exchange it was kept at a minimum on account of such social considerations as the rank of the people involved and the fact of kinship. In barter, which took place only with people of another tribe, bargaining was of prime importance. We shall, however, deal with this element of exchange in the following chapter.

VII

TRADE

While there is no doubt that trade (*wutsisex*) formed an important feature of Tlingit economy, it is difficult, at this late date, to estimate its exact significance. Remains of the material culture gathered at different villages show a surprising variety of tools, weapons, wearing apparel, and ceremonial gear. Early Russian, English, and American traders were unanimous in attesting to the definite trading procedure and the keen trading sense of the Tlingit, especially as compared with the Aleuts and other Eskimoid peoples of southern Alaska (Bancroft 1886). Iron and the knowledge of its use was found among the Tlingit by Captain Cook and Ishmailoff, the first traders to make face to face contact with these Indians (ibid.).

On being questioned about this matter the modern Tlingit hastens to say that trading was a very important occupation and was carried on, in the early days, by the *yitsati* ("keeper of the house"). It was the *yitsati* who, with the aid of his brothers, sisters' sons, and slaves, accumulated trade goods and undertook trading expeditions either to the other islands or to the tribes to the south, like the Haida or Tsimshian, or, if he lived on one of the rivers of the mainland, into the interior to trade with the Athapascan-speaking peoples.

These trading expeditions were of no mean proportions. On both land and sea great distances had to be traveled. The Sitka, Hoonah, and Klukwan villagers had to travel about three hundred miles to reach the Haida and Tsimshian, and in the fur-trading days they even undertook voyages of a thousand miles to the Victoria and Puget Sound trading posts. Even in their large and well-manned canoes, weather was a constant source of danger. Trading expeditions generally took place in May, June, and July when strong westerly winds blew constantly. (Trading was undertaken at this time because the important food gathering activities of hunting and fishing had to begin in July, or with the first run of salmon. Furthermore, when furs became an important article of trade, the winter's fur supply was available to the first trader that came along with the right trade goods.)

Hostile clans were another source of worry to the Tlingit trader. The ninety year feud between the Sitka and Wrangell people greatly hampered the trade of the Tlingit villages. Along the coast trading was thus wrought with much difficulty, and many an expedition never returned to its home village. Tlingit songs now tell of the adventures and difficulties of these early traders.

On the mainland trading with the Gonana (Athapascan) Indians was much safer as far as human relations were concerned, as the Tlingit practically dominated their neighbors of the interior. Natural obstacles were here, perhaps, even greater than on the sea. Trading expeditions into the interior took place in May, or as soon as the rivers had opened and the snow had disappeared from the lower levels. But snow slides, glaciers, and the precipitous passes were a constant source of danger to the trader. All goods had to be packed into the interior on the backs of men—generally slaves. A large basket-work sack with shoulder straps and tump line formed the pack sack of the Tlingit traders. Indians claim that a good packer could manage a hundred pounds even on a steep, dangerous incline.

Another important feature of Tlingit trade was the monopoly which certain clans and villages had on the trade routes into the interior. The Wrangell clans held all trading rights with the Athapascans at the headwaters of the Stikine River. The same was true of the Taku clans on the Taku River and the Chilcat clans on the Chilcat River. The right to import copper from the Copper River was held by the Tluk'naxadi clan of Sitka, Protecting trading rights was one of the few things which drew the often conflicting clans of the mainland villages together. On the islands, however, trading rights remained in the hands of the clans but were generally more nominal than actual. These trading rights were taken more seriously by the more powerful villages. Both the Wrangell and Klukwan villages protested strongly when the American traders began to use their trade routes. In fact, many groups of white men went into the interior on a trading expedition and never returned. When the Hudson's Bay Company set up a trading post in the Yukon Valley in 1854, the Chilcats sent a war party hundreds of miles into the interior and destroyed the post, making such an impression on the Hudson's Bay officials that it was years before it was rebuilt (Emmons 1916).

Before the arrival of white men, pure barter did not exist among the Tlingit. Exchanges took the form of gifts. But with the spread of the fur trade the Tlingit began to trade among themselves. Trade was largely intervillage and intertribal. Each house-group tended to supply its own wants by production and through trade with outside villages. This was more true of the island Tlingit than of those living on the mainland where trading became more of a profession. Often house-groups would send a representative with a trading party of some important trader of their own village, or they would give their goods to him and wait for the trader's return and payment.

The materials traded were the outcome of regional differentiation. The mainland villagers living in the river valleys were in a different ecological area than the villagers of the warmer, moister, and more heavily wooded islands. In the long, cold, damp winters the Tlingit wore fur and hide clothing. The best furs and hides for these purposes were obtained on the mainland, and these villages specialized in the making of rabbit and marmot skin blankets, moose hide shirts, trousers with stockings attached, leggings, and moccasins. Hides for the making of these articles were also prepared and exchanged. These hides and furs were in considerable demand on the islands where rabbit, marmot, and moose did not exist. Deer hides, while used on the islands, were inferior to those of the moose and caribou. In the way of food, the mainland villages produced the highly prized eulachon oil, dried eulachon, and cranberries preserved in oil. Of manufactured articles, mainland villagers produced spoons from the horns of Rocky Mountain goat and big horn sheep. Probably the best article of trade of the mainlanders was the Chilcat blanket made from cedar bark and the wool of the mountain goat. Spruce root baskets decorated with porcupine quills were also a product of this region.

In exchange for these commodities, the islanders produced dried venison, seal oil, dried halibut, dried king salmon, dried herring, dried algae, clams, mussels, sea urchins, preserved herring spawn, and numerous other sea products. They also produced cedar bark for the manufacture of the Chilcat blanket, yew wood for bows, boxes, and batons, water-tight baskets of cedar bark, green stone for tool making, and cedar wood, both red and yellow, for the making of ceremonial articles.

The mainland people also carried on a lively trade with the interior people for prepared moose hides, highly decorated moccasins, birch wood bows wound with porcupine gut, and prepared caribou hides. These hides were of the highest value in the making of shirts and trousers owing to their fine texture and durability, and all Tlingit villages provided a ready market. Thongs and sinews of various kinds were made by the interior Athapascans for sewing, binding, and the making of snowshoes. Many of the interior group were near sources of placer copper which they hammered into sheets and traded to the Tlingit. The best-known sources were in the valleys of the Copper and White rivers. In exchange the Athapascans took cedar bark baskets, fish oil, iron, and shell ornaments. When white traders appeared on the coast, fur trade between the Indians was immensely stimulated. The Tlingit secured furs not only by hunting and trapping but also by trade. Under these circumstances the Tlingit trader would take powder and shot, woolen blankets, beads, iron kettles, knives, and axes into the interior and trade for fox, beaver, marten, otter, and weasel pelts. These pelts, in turn, the Tlingit either traded to the white men who visited their villages every summer, or took them to the trading posts themselves. The trade with the Tsimshian and Haida consisted chiefly of hides, Chilcat blankets, and copper, which were exchanged for large cedar canoes, slaves, and shell ornaments.

Slave trade was particularly practiced by the Tsimshian and Haida. They either bartered for the slaves from the Kwakiutl, who in turn raided the villages of Puget Sound and the mouth of the Fraser River, or they made their own raids into this territory. While any person captured in war could be made a slave, and there were a number of Tsimshian, Haida, and even Tlingit slaves among the Tlingit, yet the greater number of slaves came from the Salish country. The chief reason for this was the fact that the slaves from the south found it almost impossible to escape and were dependable when once bought. This, of course, was not true of the Tsimshian, Haida, and Tlingit slaves who constantly escaped through the aid of their relatives and friends. Slaves also served as trade goods between the various Tlingit villages. They were readily accepted and formed, in fact, a medium of exchange. Slaves were neither taken nor bought from the interior Athapascans.

It is difficult to measure the degree of interdependence between the various house-groups and villages and the neighboring tribes. Such articles as copper shields, Chilcat blankets, and abalone shell ornaments were of the highest value in potlatch proceedings, yet these articles were produced in special regions. Wearing apparel, such as moose and caribou hide shirts, trousers with stockings attached, and moccasins were universally used by the Tlingit, yet there were no moose on the islands and certainly the greater part of the people lived on the islands. Deer were plentiful on the islands, but deer hide was inferior to that of the moose and caribou. Eulachon oil was universally used and preferred to seal oil, yet it was produced only on the mainland. The Tsimshian on the Nass and the Skeena rivers specialized in making this oil and produced a quality that was demanded by all. From both the south and the north, Indians came to trade for this oil, and the so-called grease trails into the interior were really highways of early trade. The large cedar canoes used by the Tlingit were almost invariably made by the Haida and Tsimshian, for the large red cedar (*Thuja gigantia*) used in their construction grows to the required size only south of latitude 54°40′.

Against the integrating forces of trade there existed the political unity of the clans, their rivalries and open conflicts, and monopolies of certain villages over spheres of trade. At present there is no way to measure the degree of economic interdependence of the Tlingit among themselves and with their neighbors. All that we can say is that they were a trading people, wealth was of great importance to them, and all that remains of material culture and ethnographic reports of early travelers shows that material objects of wealth were spread far from their place of origin.

Although it would not be correct to say that the Tlingit considered trade a sacred enterprise, there was some ceremonial attached to it. Preparation for a trading expedition was accompanied by certain rituals, such as fasting for luck, getting a shaman to foretell the future, and holding a feast and dance several days before departure. The traders sometimes painted their faces as if going to war, but it is not certain whether this was connected with trade itself or was done to insure protection against enemies on the way. The return of a successful trading party was an occasion for feasting and dancing.

The trader generally had definite trading connections with individuals at other villages or in neighboring tribes. On his arrival he would be met with a certain amount of ceremony and led to the house of his business associate. Exchanges were made publicly accompanied by a great deal of haggling. Each side set its prices high and then came down to a level where exchange was possible. Lesser traders and representatives of other house-groups bartered on the side. The whole proceeding smacked very much of a marketplace. When the party was small and the house chief bartered for the group as a whole, his every act was carefully watched by his kinsmen. Quite often a shrewd old woman was taken along who kept a check on exchange values. The two leaders would call out the values of the goods to be exchanged in rotation and, when the price suited the group behind each leader, a shout would go up signifying that exchange was agreeable at that point.

While trading relations were friendly and semiceremonial, traders did not hesitate to trick and cheat one another. This was particularly true of the traders going into the interior. When firearms first came into use, the interior people were very anxious to secure them and gave their furs indiscriminately. Indians now tell of how they obtained flintlocks from the white traders for a pile of furs equal to the height of the gun and then traded the same gun to the Athapascans for a pile of furs twice the height of the gun. They also tell stories of how they dyed red fox furs black in an effort to delude the white trader. If caught cheating, the Indian did not feel ashamed, laughing it off as a good joke.

White traders soon became aware of the deceiving qualities of the Indian trader and protected one another by giving letters of recommendation to the Indian trading notabilities which they were to show to any trader that came along. The Indian was impressed by these bits of paper and believed that they added to his prestige, and on potlatch occasions he exhibited them among his crests. It is said that even today some of these letters exist among the old Tlingits who cherish them as priceless valuables. If the Indian had been able to read the contents of these letters, not very many of them would have been kept, for quite a number described the possessor as the biggest crook and liar in southeastern Alaska and still others made humorous remarks about the person of the Indian or told of some event which the writer had experienced in the village.

The exchange values of Tlingit society were as clear in the minds of the Tlingits as were their religious, moral, and esthetic values. Each article was valued in terms of articles placed against it in barter. It would be idle here to question the elements that went into making up the exchange value of some article. Certainly costs and the subjective valuations of the traders working unconsciously set what valuations they made. These in turn were but functions of the entire economic value system of their social milieu. It is important to note that the coming of the white man changed the economic value pattern of the Tlingit. For instance, before the advent of the white man the Indian valued furs in the following order: sea otter, marten, beaver, otter, black fox, cross fox, mink, wolverine, wolf, and bear. The sea otter was the highest and the bear was the lowest in value. White traders set the following sequence: sea otter, black fox, cross fox, beaver, marten, otter, mink, wolf, wolverine, and bear. The sea otter appealed to the Indian as it did to the Chinese mandarin and the European aristocrat. The fur of the sea otter was of ideal size, reaching from the shoulder to the ankle. The fur was fine, glossy, dark brown, extremely durable, and warm. Hence the general demand for it, and the fact that the sea otter has gone the way of the American bison and the passenger pigeon.

What exchange values were for the general run of commodities before the advent of the whites is not in the memory of the oldest Indian. But many old men remember the exchanges made in terms of white man's trade goods. The following will illustrate some of these:

1 marten fur—10 lead shots in a bag
1 gun—a pile of furs equal to it in height
2 black fox furs—1 breech loading gun
2 black fox furs—1 Chilcat blanket

1 large canoe—$150.00 [1]

1 slave—25 otter pelts; 2 sea otter pelts; 4 Chilcat blankets; 10 to 15 moose hides [2]

1 extra large canoe—10 to 15 slaves [3]

Supply and demand seem to have influenced the exchange value of goods. Old men speak of having to give away eulachon oil for next to nothing when extra large runs of these fish visited the entire coast. Monopoly rights in trade were also maintained in order to keep up the exchange values. Dentalium shells, which the Russians introduced as a medium of exchange, offer another example of supply and demand. When English and American traders discovered that dentalium shells were used as money, they immediately brought in vast quantities from the coast of California and the Columbia River region where these shells abounded. So plentiful did dentalium become that it has lost its value completely among the Tlingit.

In conclusion we can make several useful generalizations from the study of Tlingit trade. From the point of view of exchange the Tlingit have a barter economy. While it is true that abalone shells, dentalium shells, and furs formed media of exchange before European contact, they were of minor importance as compared with the direct exchange of one type of goods for another. Even with the advent of the woolen blanket, the gun, powder, and shot as media of exchange, direct exchange of goods or barter took care of by far the greater portion of exchanges.

An important fact to remember also is that exchange values were definitely known. The amount of one commodity that should be exchanged for a certain amount of another was a matter of custom. Individual or subjective elements tended to be ruled out. When the white man arrived on the scene with a number of new articles, there was, at first, a breakdown of exchange values in terms of these new articles. The subjective value was for a time predominant, and there were as many exchange values for

1. "In Holmberg's time a large, so-called war canoe had a value of eight hundred Banco-Rubles in Russian merchandise, and now the Americans pay up to one hundred fifty dollars for the larger ones." Aurel Krause, *Die Tlingit Indianer* (1885), trans. by Erna Gunther, *The Tlingit Indians* (Seattle: University of Washington Press, 1956), p. 119.

2. Ibid., p. 132 (quoting Feodor Lutke).

3. Ibid.

an article as there were traders. But a stable level was soon reached which tended to perpetuate itself.

The Tlingit trader of the old days was extremely interested in getting the best possible value for his goods. If he heard that a white trader some distance off offered a bit more than he was offered near his home, he would take his furs to the highest bidder no matter if it took him and his friends a week or two to go there and come back—another example indicating that time is of little importance to the Tlingit.

A clear definition of the relationship of kinship and trade has also to be made. True barter with its characteristics of bargaining was found primarily between the Tlingit and his non-Tlingit neighbors. When the house-group took advantage of the specialized skill of one of its members, this member's needs were taken care of automatically by the house-group. There was exchange, however, within the house-group of the products of handicrafts which were, for the most part, individual property. This exchange took the form of a gift which has been discussed in the chapter on distribution.

Regional distribution of resources resulted in regional specialization of production and in regional interdependence. Individual specialization resulted in the mutual interdependence of individuals. From this situation arose a certain degree of economic integration, the extent of which is now difficult to ascertain. While the Tlingit house-group did not produce for a market but for its own maintenance, it was by no means self-sustaining. The phratral duties of house building and the making of ceremonial articles involved the village. To these must be added the need for the products of the handicrafts and foods from other regions. It seems, therefore, that we have here a household economy with numerous and strong lines of attachment through exchange to the other members of the village and less numerous lines to other villages. It must, however, always be remembered that these economic connections were individual connections between house-chiefs or lesser members of a house. The extensive, numerous, and multiform connections through a market did not exist.

VIII

THE CONSUMPTION OF WEALTH

Household Consumption

The house-group produces the basic necessities in common, and these necessities are consumed in common. In the morning the women boil fresh salmon, trout, or cod on the central fire. Each member of the house then ladles out his or her portion from the cooking box onto a wooden platter. As a rule boiled fish is sufficient for breakfast, which is eaten about eight o'clock in the morning. If guests are present or a long journey is ahead, fish is followed by fresh or preserved berries. In the old days the Tlingit used no drink but water.

Late in the afternoon the men return from their various tasks and have their big meal of the day. This consists of dried or smoked salmon toasted before the fire and dipped in eulachon oil. Dried salmon is the staple diet of the Tlingit as it is of the other Northwest Coast Indians. It is undoubtedly very nourishing and provides a balanced diet. Besides, it is easily packed in boxes or baskets and presents little difficulty in transportation. When the Tlingit are on the trail or on long sea voyages dried salmon is often the sole diet. The usual way to eat dried fish is for each person to break off a piece and dip it in the oil dish, which is situated in the center of a group of eaters. After this main dish of dried fish, the Tlingit eat dried seaweed chipped up and mixed in oil; then come berries, roots, or stems, fresh or preserved. Drinking water is passed around during the meal. Shellfish, fresh or dried, may be substituted for dried salmon. Meat is not very common and is considered more a delicacy than a necessity.

Mountain goat meat on the mainland and venison on the islands form the chief meat supply. Grouse, ducks, and geese are, of course, welcome whenever obtainable.

There are only two regular meals for the day, breakfast and dinner. Children eat whenever they can, which is most of the day. In the summer when the evenings are long, people often help themselves to whatever they can find around the house. In the early summer when the fresh stalks, roots, and berries appear, young people spend much of their time feeding in the bushes about the village. A little later, trips lasting over several days are made, especially by the young people, to islands where the sea gulls nest. Eggs are boiled and eaten on the spot and are also brought home in great quantities.

There is always plenty of food in the house; no one ever needs to go hungry. Individual tastes can be satisfied by going fishing or hunting whenever a large enterprise is not under way. It is the common belief of white people that the Indian's diet is tasteless and lacks variety. Nothing is further from the truth. The food of the Tlingit is rich and varied and is artfully prepared. Every old Tlingit speaks with disgust of the white man's food and emphasizes the delicacy of his own. Comparing the foods of the old Tlingit with the poor bread, tea, coffee, and canned goods of the younger generation, one is at once made aware of the greater nourishing capacity of the former. Few foods are more tasty to the writer than fresh salmon broiled, Indian fashion, before a fire or the boiled roots of the camas and allied plants. Fish oil, on account of its smell, does not appeal to the palate of the white man but cannot be said to be more repulsive than various old cheeses.

The Tlingit eat about the same quantity as white people although at feasts they could probably out-eat most whites. In the consumption of oil the Indian is far ahead of the white man. A pint of oil a day is not considered overmuch for a hard working Indian. When first introduced to butter an Indian would consume most of a pound at one meal.

On account of the cool, damp climate, the Tlingit formerly wore shirts and trousers of buckskin or moose hide. In the summer the trousers were often discarded and a long shirt was considered sufficient. Moccasins were used in winter but during the hot weather the Tlingit went barefooted. Tightly woven cedar bark hats were used by everyone. Robes made from the furs of the sea otter, marten, land otter, and wolf were worn in winter and on ceremonial occasions by the wealthy. Poor people made fur robes of bear, rabbit, and marmot skins. Robes were often made from cedar bark, especially for women and children. The Chilcat blanket was worn only on ceremonial occasions.

Women used buckskin shirts and short trousers over which they wore a mantle woven from soft cedar bark. When in the house they went barefooted. Children wore long shirts of buckskin in winter but in summer they often went entirely naked.

The shelter of the Tlingit was formerly provided by their wooden houses, and according to white man's standards these houses were very warm and comfortable. The floor was always a foot or two below the surface of the earth and often several feet below it. This did away with drafts and held the warm air close to the floor. In time one grows accustomed to the smoke but the eyes are injured. It is a common observation that most Tlingit past middle age have poor eyesight and that very few reach advanced age without blindness. The Tlingit slept on raised platforms near the walls, in former days, using fur robes as covers. There seems little doubt that they were warm enough. The houses were not over clean from the white man's point of view. Fish oil and soot are a bad combination in any house, and where there is no soap they become a permanent coating to everything.

The Potlatch

As the utilization of wealth is of primary importance in the potlatch, we begin our discussion with a treatment of potlatch goods. Before the coming of the white men, the articles exclusively used were slaves and coppers. Slaves, as has already been pointed out, were captured in raids or purchased from the southern tribes, these slaves being generally Salish Indians from Puget Sound. Every wealthy house had a certain number of slaves to perform its menial tasks and to be the servants of the *yitsati* ("keeper of the house") and his immediate family. These household slaves were never very numerous, ten being considered a large number. The slaves to be used at a potlatch were, on the other hand, always purchased immediately before the occasion and were not used for the purposes of economic services. Before great potlatches the giver would send out his nephews to buy slaves from the south and to bring them back to the village where they were well looked after until the time for their use arrived. Men, women, and children were accepted as potlatch slaves although men were more highly valued.

During the potlatch, these slaves were either killed, freed, or given away as presents. The Tlingit say that the earliest method was that of killing, the slaves being ceremonially killed before the house of the host with a special picklike instrument made from a whale's rib. The bodies were then thrown into the sea. Much more common was the practice, during the Russian occupation of Alaska, of freeing the slaves. The climax of the potlatch was reached when the host would free the slaves he had bought for the occasion. These slaves were then free men and could settle in the village of their late master. These freed slaves married either women in the same position as themselves or even Tlingit women. Many of the house-groups of low status among the Tlingit originated in this manner. Of lesser importance was the giving of slaves as presents. It took place in a small potlatch within a single village. But in the great intervillage potlatches slaves were not given away.

The copper (*tinnah*) was the popular article until the turn of the century, when it was replaced by money and woolen blankets. The copper was beaten out of placer copper found in the interior of Alaska. The Athapascan Indians brought it to the coast where it was taken by the Tlingit in exchange for cedar bark baskets and fish oil. These rough copper plates were then shaped by the Tlingit into shieldlike objects and covered with drawings of animals and birds. Some were very large, as high as six feet. Others, again, could be covered by the palm of the hand. The average size of a copper was about two feet long by a foot and a half wide, the weight being from thirty to forty pounds. A copper of this size was valued at five or six slaves.

In contrast to the tribes to the south, the copper varied very little in value among the Tlingit. Age did not make any difference. If a copper was broken and a piece thrown into the sea, it increased in value equal to the part thrown away. That is, if half was thrown away the copper was worth one and a half times as much as originally. The copper among the Tlingit was not considered to possess ritual significance as it did among the

Kwakiutl, where its value increased with age and the number of times it passed hands. The Tlingit considered the copper as concentrated wealth, a symbol equal to so much fish oil, or whatever was given for it in exchange.

In recent times blankets have been used, the unit being the woolen double blanket of the type popularized in the north by the Hudson's Bay Company. The Indians are forced to buy these blankets at the current market prices, but once in circulation among themselves these blankets remain fixed in value. Finally, there is currency, either gold, silver, or paper, which is now most popular. The blankets and money used for potlatching are never used for economic purposes. The blankets are stored away in large cedar chests and eventually wear out by exchange and transportation or are eaten up by moths. A Tlingit would never consider using these blankets for keeping his back warm. Potlatch money, likewise, is kept hidden away, and many a young Tlingit today is looking for the "pot of gold" which he believes his dead uncle buried somewhere near the village.

The true potlatch goods, then, are slaves, coppers, blankets, and money. These goods are never used for economic purposes and must be clearly distinguished, on the one hand, from the economic goods in everyday use, and, on the other, from the totemic crests and emblems to which they give value. Potlatch goods are derived from the surplus of economic goods through exchange, this surplus, in turn, arising from an excess of work over that required for purely economic needs.

If these economic goods circulated from one individual to another, then no great demand would be placed on the productive capacity of the society. In actual practice, however, we have to recognize first that a great number of slaves were freed, that great numbers of coppers were thrown into the sea, and that great numbers of blankets were torn up and pieces given away as mementos of the occasion; second, that there was a constant endeavor to give greater potlatches which, in turn, demanded increased production. Finally, there was the practice of borrowing. When a house-group decided to give a potlatch, it set about accumulating potlatch goods with the aid of the entire local clan division. Even the combined efforts of the local clan division would not be sufficient, so the sponsoring house would often borrow from the clans of its own phratry. These debts were paid back with approximately 20 percent interest. There was no definite time limit. For every four blankets, five would be paid back. If the debtor did not pay his debts within a reasonable time, his creditor would bring him to terms by having him publicly ridiculed through songs and stories or by making a copy of his clan totem. This was considered a great insult and the debtor's clansmen did their best to settle the debt. If a debtor's clansmen repaid the debt, he would become a debt slave until such time as he had fully repaid the debt.

In more recent times one could borrow from people of the opposite side, most generally from one's brothers-in-law. These potlatch debts which were purely economic became more and more extensive and complex. With the prevailing interest rates, lending became an accredited method of investment. Many writers have confused these economic debt obligations with the potlatch obligations. The two are quite separate. While it is true that the debts are incurred in the form of gifts, it is not a potlatch gift but one following the pattern of the exchange of economic goods.

The early practice was to borrow fish oil, furs, money, and ornaments and to use them in purchasing slaves, coppers, and blankets. Later, blankets and money were borrowed outright and used as potlatch gifts. But the distinction between the purely economic transaction of borrowing and lending and the ceremonial exchange in the potlatch still remained. Blankets could be borrowed and returned with interest, being ends in a commercial transaction, but in the potlatch these same blankets would become means to important social values.

No discussion of potlatch goods would be complete without some mention of the ceremonial paraphernalia used on the occasion. The so-called potlatch ceremony falls into three main parts: the feast; the dances, songs, and theatricals; and the presentation of the ceremonial gifts. The foods used in the feast are those already mentioned in production. During a potlatch there must be great supplies of food, more, in fact, than could be used. The ceremonial gear consists of the robes, masks, hats, rattles, and batons. Chilcat blankets are worn by the chiefs and head men while lesser people wear blankets covered with large pearl buttons. Wooden masks representing mythical and real ancestors were worn by dancers in representing the adventures of the clan. Rattles made in the form of birds, with a few pebbles inside, are used to beat time in the dances. The drum, made by stretching rawhide over a hollow piece of log, is always present in the ceremony. Dance leaders use long flat pieces of wood, carved and painted with clan emblems. These batons inform the audience which clan is performing and which special ceremonial is to be enacted. All dancers wear hats or head ornaments of various forms. These hats often represent the emblems of the clan and house, and even the phratry. They are not the sacred totemic objects around which the presentation of goods took place but were the private property of the individuals using them.

To sum up our analysis of the material aspect of the potlatch, there are, first, the food consumed in the feast and the goods used for the accumulation of the gifts. These goods constitute the economic surplus. Second, there are the ceremonial paraphernalia and dress used in the performances. These articles are not made directly for use in any potlatch but are part of the general ceremonial life of the people. Third, there are the real potlatch goods such as slaves, coppers, blankets, and money. Fourth, there are the totemic emblems and crests represented by the hats worn by the chiefs and head men of the various clans present. These clan and house crests are the objects to which potlatch goods give value and are, therefore, central in the whole process of potlatching. I shall later deal more fully with the relationship between these crests and the gift giving. It is here necessary only to keep in mind that they are part of the material equipment of the potlatch.

We have already noted that potlatches occur on such occasions as the completion of house building, burial, and the preparation of the young for adult life. But potlatches also occur whenever an individual, house, or clan believes that it is rich enough to give one. It seems that originally potlatches were always associated with the important events in social life, but that, as the accumulation of wealth owing to white contact became easier, potlatching tended to become an end in itself. However, a potlatch is never given without some reason. The two reasons most commonly given for potlatches not connected with social events are the honoring of the dead and the honoring of children. A wealthy house can decide on a potlatch. If it is of very high rank, it tends to honor its ancestors, but if it is of low rank and wishes to raise its status, it honors its children. A potlatch is often given in honor of a promising young clansman or clanswoman. Potlatches are thus given whenever a local clan group feels itself rich enough to do so, and it is a simple matter to find a reason for the occasion. The natives themselves distinguish between the potlatches connected with the important events of life and those which are purely for the display of wealth and the enhancement of prestige. Potlatches connected with house building, burial, and the preparation of the young for adult life are known as *xu'ix*, but those given for prestige are known as *tutxu'ix*. Formally they are the same. In both cases the giver and his clansmen gain prestige. In the *xu'ix* the ceremonial exchange of gifts is intimately connected with the ceremonial exchange of services. It is a part of a series of interphratral reciprocities within a village in which the elements of cooperation and solidarity seem to be paramount. In the *tutxu'ix*, however, the guests come from other villages. The underlying tone is that of competition and self-aggrandizement. It is given in order to honor clan members, not to commemorate important social events within the village. Economically, both are ways of using wealth, although in the *tutxu'ix* in destruction of wealth is large.

As soon as a *tutxu'ix* is decided upon by a house-group, all other houses of the local clan have to be consulted as their help is essential. Then the clansmen in the nearest villages are informed and their opinion and help sought. Finally, the village as a whole has to agree to become the hosts for the visiting clans. The selection of guests is always a matter of the greatest importance. The primary purpose is to return all the potlatches which the giver has himself attended. As he cannot cancel all his obligations in one potlatch, he has to select the visitors in accordance with his immediate capacity to pay. To be able to give seven potlatches in one's lifetime is considered the highest honor: no one is known to have exceeded that number. While several local clans of the opposite side are invited and share in the feasting and dancing, only the chiefs and those who have given the host gifts in the past receive presents.

Sending out invitations takes place months in advance. The nephews of the chief about to give a potlatch are sent to the neighboring villages. When the canoe reaches the village, the young men call out their message so that the whole village can hear it. They then land and are escorted to the houses of their future visitors where they are feasted for a number of days. No one ever refuses an invitation to a potlatch, for to do so is tantamount to refusing a gift—an unpardonable insult. However, very important people have to be invited several times before they accept.

The reception of potlatch guests is always a grand affair. Before landing, the visitors give long speeches, extolling the merits of their hosts. The latter in turn reply. Then, after the firing of many guns and the blowing of horns, the landing is made. A man at the door of the host's house calls out the name of each important guest, only honorific names being used. The head of the house, standing before the screen opposite the doorway, calls out, "Be seated where you always belong." One of the young men then leads the visitor to his seat. Seating is one of the most difficult tasks of the host, for by seating, the rank of the visitor is made public. If it were only a matter of descent, it would be a simple task, but potlatching constantly shifts the relative importance of chiefs. Long and bitter feuds have often arisen over the question of seating. If a host wishes to insult one of his rivals, he offers him a seat in one of the corners. An important man would never accept such a seat and would leave in anger. If a guest is thus angered by mistake, the host pacifies him with gifts and eventually seats him in a place befitting his dignity and honor. The highest honor that a host can pay a guest at a potlatch is to offer him his seat at the head of the house.

According to strict custom, a potlatch is a four-day affair. On the first day, speech making by both sides, feasting, and dancing by the hosts take place. Before every feast, large bowls of water in which the people wash their hands are passed around. The nephews of the host act as waiters. The first course is dried salmon, toasted before the fire and passed around on wooden platters. A man follows with an oil dish into which each guest dips his piece of fish. The visitor of highest rank always receives the first dish. Various kinds of seaweeds, dried and mixed in oil, follow. Then come boiled clams, sea urchins, and mussels, followed by fresh or preserved salmonberry stalks and other succulent roots and stems. Finally there are berries mixed in oil, the greatest delicacy being soapberries mashed and beaten into a white creamy froth. The entire meal takes from three to five hours and is interlarded with speeches and jokes. The women are not formally treated although they are within the feast ring. They eat, listen, and keep silent. The children are in the background.

On the second day the visitors perform dances belonging to their clans for the pleasure of their hosts and feasting continues. Their totemic crests are displayed and their origin and importance explained.

The third day is given up to theatricals and contests of various kinds, and begins with an eating contest in which both guests and hosts participate. One of the main features is a fish oil drinking contest. Imitations of other people's dances and customs follow. Another important feature is the contests between rival shamans, each endeavoring to perform the most miraculous conjuring act, such as walking through fire or shooting arrows at a robe without piercing it. During these contests the audience watch the performers with the greatest intensity. If anyone makes a mistake, he is jeered and hooted at. So intense is the effort on the part of the actors that they often collapse from shame if they make a slight error in the performance, and it is said that some have even died. The culmination of the potlatch occurs on the fourth day, which is given over to making presentations. Everyone dresses in his best and displays all the crests to which he has a right. The giver of the potlatch stands before the screen or the door of his house, a great pile of goods beside him. He calls out the names of the visitors to whom gifts are to be given. The man of highest rank comes first and he receives the greatest gift. The host's nephews act as go-betweens. The guests let one of their less important kinsmen receive the gifts, they, themselves, standing around, looking as unconcerned as possible. If the host has much food, he will keep his guests for a week or even longer before giving them the potlatch gifts. It was not uncommon for a host to take his guests on a hunting trip or for short visits to nearby villages. After whisky was introduced among the Indians, potlatches often deteriorated into long drunken orgies, the whole affair ending either in a fight or when all the liquor had been consumed.

Potlatching takes place in most villages every summer and every winter. June and July are potlatching months as were November and December. All the people of the host village attend the potlatch and take part in the feasting and the dancing. They do not all get potlatch gifts. Everyone attending a potlatch receives a piece of blanket for witnessing the event. Every invited guest receives a badge which signifies that he has received a gift from his host. The host himself puts another ring on his cedar bark potlatch hat which he wears on the top of his clan crest hat.

The people concerned in a potlatch can be separated into categories according to the part they play in the proceedings. First, there is the giver of the potlatch who is the *yitsati* ("keeper of the house") of some important house. His house-group supports him in making the event a success. Then comes his local clan division which also supports him and is present at the potlatch. Clansmen from other villages often help and attend, but this may not be always necessary. Second, a prestige potlatch, *tutx̱u'ix̱*, is always dedicated to someone, either a dead ancestor or young man or woman of the clan. Third, there are the invited guests who are always from the opposite phratry. The invitations are sent to the house chiefs, but they always bring their households with them. The principle is to invite the clan, but, as many clan houses are of low rank, they are conveniently left out. Fourth, there are all the people of the host's village who participate in the feasting and dancing, and who receive some token for being present but whose presence is not essential to the potlatch. Slaves took no part in the potlatch, not even as servers; they were used only as property.

The totemic crests are intimately connected with the potlatch proceedings. In the chapter on social organization I have pointed out the relationship of these crests or emblems to the house-group, clan, and phratry. The popular way of representing a totem is in the form of a hat. Each clan has one of these hats which is higher in value than any of its other totems. In the Raven phratry, for instance, every Raven hat represents the Raven totem, but each hat has a slightly different form and a distinct name. It is these formalized symbols of the totem that I have called crests or emblems.

To the Tlingit, rank and prestige are of primary importance, and the acquisition of this social value is dependent upon cooperation. No house chief is able to give a great potlatch without the help of the other houses of his clan. While the primary motive is one of personal prestige and power, in actual practice it becomes translated into clan prestige and clan power. The clan crest is the symbol which combines the ambitions of the individual with those of his group; to elevate yourself you elevate your clan.

The Tlingit, in common with the other Northwest Coast people, measure rank in terms of wealth. An individual is worth the bride gift of his mother. A clan is worth the amount of wealth given at its last potlatch added to its former prestige value. The measure of clan value, the medium through which it is expressed, is the crest. The value of the crest is the value of the clan, and the potlatch is the mechanism through which the crest is given value. The value of a clan may be distributed over several crests or it may be concentrated in one. The giver of the potlatch has to decide which crest or crests he wishes to use, and in this he is influenced by the amount of wealth he has available and the opinion of his clansmen. The clan, as we know, is made up of a number of house-groups, and one of these houses is of paramount importance. In this house resides the *ankaua* ("rich man") and the sacred crests. If the local clan division is large and contains many houses, it often happens that one of the houses of lesser importance wishes to give a potlatch on a grand scale. This house has the right to demand any of the clan crests that it wishes to display, and the trustees of the crests will have to let them be thus used. The crests have definite value and, if the trustees and the clansmen generally do not think that the prospective potlatch giver has enough goods, they may refuse to give him the clan crest or crests. Disputes of this nature often occurred within the clan. The Tluk'naxadi clan of Sitka have two Raven hats, one being the original, and the other a hat made by one of the house-groups who grew to great power in historic times. There was an effort to prevent this house-group from getting too far ahead of the others by refusing to let it use the hat, but it was strong enough to defy the clan members and to make a hat of its own. At present the house has waned in power and its hat has now become an accredited subsidiary crest of the Tluk'naxadi. Disputes over crests also arose between clans of the same phratry. The Tluxakati and the Ganaxtedi of Chilcat carried on a feud for fourteen years over a special Raven hat. The Ganaxtedi finally won owing to superior strength, but the Tluxakati still maintain that they are the real Ravens.

Among the large clans potlatching became restricted to several of its most important house-groups. These houses claim to have the sole right to represent the clan. They call themselves the *anyeti*—a class of people possessing considerable wealth and holding the honorific titles of the clan. They maintain that they are *anyeti* because their ancestors gave great potlatches in the past. Thus the restriction of potlatch giving to a certain class has tended to diminish the constant friction existing between a number of competing houses.

The rank of the local clan division depends upon the value of its crests. This value is shared by all the clan members but particularly by the *anyeti* of the clan. The rank of a house within the local clan division depends upon the potlatches it has initiated. The values of the crests are created at a potlatch when the giver displays the crest while making the presentations. The names of the crest hats often reveal their value. "Slaves-half-way-around-the-room," "Slaves-all-the-way-around-the-room," "Two-coppers-facing-one-another," "A-stack-of-blankets-gun-high," are some of the names of the crests. The crest has a permanent name besides these names which change at each potlatch.

The sponsor of a potlatch may give value to as many crests as he wishes. The Tluk'naxadi of Sitka have the salmon, cow, and raven as emblems. A giver of a potlatch can use them all, although the common practice is to value the Raven emblem. A poor house often takes one of the less valuable emblems and by displaying it gains prestige which it could never hope to get if it had to display the Raven emblem.

When the presentations are made, the giver of the potlatch either wears the crests on his person or has one of his kinsmen hold it above his head. The crests or crest have to be clearly visible and closely connected with the body of the giver during the time of the presentation. If they are not so displayed, they do not get value. The potlatch goods to be given to the visitors are carefully counted out beforehand, and, as the giver of the potlatch calls out the name of his guest, a kinsman calls out the amount of the gift. In the old days, when slaves were killed or freed, the giver called out the number, and his kinsman marched the slaves before the visitors and out to slaughter or to freedom. Coppers were either given as presents or thrown away whole or bit by bit.

There is tense excitement during the presentation. All present make mental note of how much each person has received. A potlatch, as a rule, cancels not only old debts but creates new credits. After the gifts have been distributed, blankets are torn up and pieces given to those who did not receive gifts. The potlatch is then officially over, and the guests depart, some satisfied, others jealous of the high honors given to their host, and still others disgruntled by not receiving what they expected.

It is well to emphasize here that there are four important rules which potlatch givers have to observe. The first demands that a potlatch can be given only to people on the opposite side. This rule conforms to the dual organization of the Tlingit, but it cannot be forgotten that the Haida also have a dual organization, yet one can potlatch people of one's own side. The second rule states that a potlatch must be for the purpose of displaying and elevating the totemic crests of the giver's clan; or that the potlatch be given in honor of some member of that clan. The third rule demands that only the host gives gifts. Among the Kwakiutl competitive gift giving takes place at potlatches. The fourth rule demands that a gift must be returned. No time limit is set, but six or seven years is considered ample time for one to accumulate enough wealth to give a return potlatch. This return gift must be made at a potlatch. If the gift is not returned within a reasonable time, the debtor's clan lays claim to one of the creditor clan's crests and holds it until the debt is paid.

Economic and social as the potlatch may seem, it has a definite ritual aspect. It is connected with the emblems, whose religious significance has already been indicated. The myths of the Tlingit show that the ceremonial gift was a part of the workings of their social organization. But the potlatch to which these myths refer is the one connected with the ceremonies of house building, burial, and the preparation of the young for adult life. Even today the people of the more out-of-the-way villages speak of the potlatch in these terms. In this chapter, however, I have dealt entirely with the large intervillage potlatch which is not connected with ceremonial labor. One gives a potlatch when one has accumulated sufficient wealth.

Among the Tsimshian, Haida, and Kwakiutl the potlatch is purely a social affair and so it has tended to become among the Tlingit. It is difficult to say what all the causes contributing to making the potlatch more and more a competitive institution were; but the introduction of metal tools, traps, and firearms, leading to greater material wealth, certainly played a leading part.

What is the function of the potlatch among the Tlingit? A minimum definition might define it as giving value through wealth. Its aim is to create value, to make something important and to give power and prestige. It does this by utilizing material wealth through the feast and the gift. Work, economic goods, potlatch goods, totemic crests, and group and individual prestige are the stages of development drawn together and unified in it. It begins with human effort and ends with human satisfaction through a series of transfers of value from one type of symbol to another.

By giving a potlatch the individual's need for personal honor tends to be satisfied. He gets an ancestral clan name, the value of which is socially recognized. To the little cedar bark hat, which he wears over the clan hat, he adds another ring, telling his world the number of the potlatches he has given. Songs and stories of his potlatch are carried away and are sung and told in every village of his land. He is famous, for he has succeeded in the most highly valued enterprise of his world.

The clan of the potlatch giver gives its help and receives in return crests of a higher value and additional publicity and re-nown. The visitors get a prolonged feast and entertainment, and those whose regard is highly rated, valuable gifts. For everything obtained something is given. From one point of view the pot-latch is cooperation; the house helps the head man, the clan helps the house. The gifts are eventually returned from the opposites. Along with this cooperation goes conflict. House against house, man against man, clan against clan within the same phratry are in constant competition with one another. Class restrictions are an accommodation to this conflict. Finally there is the conflict be-tween the clans of the opposite sides. Who can give away the greatest amount of wealth? What restrictions can be placed upon the economic progress of the opposite clans by monopolies in trade routes, restrictions of trapping and fishing territories, and the use of witchcraft as a means of getting rid of rivals? In the potlatch these conflicts and cooperations are held together at a high tension, making it the most vital institution in the Tlingit world.

The Bride Gift

In order to get a bride every Tlingit has to have a bride gift. Both the selection of the bride and the amount of the gift are, however, determined and arranged long before the ceremony. The young man has a choice but it is a narrow one. The factors of kinship, rank, and property guide his marital enterprises with great certainty. The young man's maternal uncle is the moving spirit in the accumulation of the bride gift, or, more accurately, the *yitsati* of the house sees that all his nephews are properly married. The bride gift thus comes out of the accumulated savings of the house-group and consists of the same things as those used in the potlatch.

If the young man is capable and energetic, he can add to his bride gift by his own efforts and endeavor to obtain a bride of higher rank than himself. As a rule, bride gifts are not very high unless, for diplomatic reasons, the house-group wishes to obtain a woman of high rank. The highest bride gift known in the last thirty years amounted to five hundred dollars.

When the time for the wedding ceremony arrives, the boy's uncle takes the bride gift to the house of the girl's uncle where he presents them to the girl's kinsmen, saying, "Do not trouble to pay us back." The girl's uncle puts the gift among his other savings or divides it up among his near kinsmen.

There is no return gift made. In this the Tlingit differ from their neighbors, the Tsimshian, Haida, and Kwakiutl, who make elaborate gift exchanges during and after a marriage ceremony. The Tlingit claim that return gifts are sometimes made but that they are of much less value than the original gift to the girl's uncle. We cannot, therefore, speak of the exchange of gifts at marriage and must look at the bride gift as fundamentally a reciprocation of the girl's kinsmen for the loss of a clan member.

If a woman died shortly after marriage, the husband could demand her sister, real or classificatory, as her successor without further payment. This would also hold true if the girl turned out badly and had to be returned to her people.

The bride gift, therefore, validates the act of marriage. It reveals and emphasizes the ranks of the young man and the young woman. It lays the responsibility for the girl's conduct on her kinsmen. It creates definite reciprocal relations between the two house-groups. From the economic point of view, the bride gift is a definite form of wealth consumption.

The Indemnity

Many offenses against the life, property, and honor of a Tlingit were settled by a payment of goods. In legal disputes, just as in the other aspects of Tlingit life, rank played the determining part. Just how a crime was to be punished depended upon the status and importance of the individual concerned. Above rank, of course, towered the imposing power of the clan. There was no central legal authority before which legal disputes could be brought. Within the clan only incest and witchcraft were punished. All other crimes were settled by the clans concerned.

Murder was generally punished by death—a man of equal rank being selected from the murderer's clan. In case the murderer was of much higher rank than the man murdered, his clan would offer restitution by a payment of goods. This would also be true if there were slight differences of rank between the murdered man and the man selected to pay for his loss. Equality was demanded and differences were always made up by payments of goods.

In case murder or other trouble led to a feud in which many people were killed, both sides finally came to agreement when equality was established. Very large payments were often made to bring about a settlement. Adultery when it occurred between people of equal rank was not taken up by the clan. The injured husband could kill his wife and the adulterer if he wished. If he was fond of his wife he could forgive her, but her clan must pay him a considerable amount to clear his honor. If the adulterer was of higher rank, the husband's own clan paid the husband property to clear his honor, as the killing of a man of high rank was a dangerous undertaking. That is to say, in cases of this sort the husband was pacified by payments of goods from both his own clan and the clan of his wife, the clan of the adulterer getting off without punishment.

If a man of low rank had unlawful sex relations with a woman of high rank, the matter was much more seriously treated. First, the wife's clansmen killed two men, between the man and woman in rank, belonging to the adulterer's clan. This was to show that the woman's clansmen were very angry and would not let the matter drop. The man's clan was then expected to offer one of its men equal in rank to the woman to be slain. If this was done, the woman's clan then offered a payment for the killing of the first two men. If this was not done a feud would follow.

The penalty for assault was payment in goods. A Tlingit of high rank was very sensitive about his appearance and if, in a dispute, someone struck him so as to cause marks on his face, he would remain indoors until the marks were healed and until a public payment had been made to him by the clan of his assaulter.

If a man accidentally shamed himself by injury, careless speech, or indecent exposure, he had to pay his clansmen for the dishonor he had brought to them.

If a man were accidentally injured by a member of his own clan, by the other man's dog, or by falling in front of or catching cold in the other man's house, the damages were always repaired by a payment of goods.

As has already been mentioned, the bride gift of the mother set the value of individuals and governed any payments that were to be made. The goods used in payment were the same kind as those used in the potlatch. Payment did not have to be made immediately in full but could be spread over a number of years. These goods came from the savings of the house-group or were augmented, in the case of important individuals, by contributions from other house-groups of the clan.

When a crime was committed representatives of the clans concerned met and discussed what was to be done. They informed their respective clans of their decision, and if the clans were satisfied a public transaction took place in which the dispute was settled either by a public execution or by the payment of goods. These preliminary discussions, the punishments, and payments had to be strictly public for their validation rested entirely upon the statement of the villagers.

Important payments were made during the peace dance which always ended a serious dispute. In the peace dance, ceremonial hostages were taken by each clan from the clan of the enemy. These hostages then danced in imitation of harmless animals and birds, like the deer, the robin, and the hummingbird. They sang in honor of the lately disputing clans and by symbolic actions and words sought to bring about good feeling. After the dance the payments were made, and the whole affair culminated in a feast.

The indemnity thus constituted an important form of wealth utilization. The clan organization was certainly not conducive to lessening the points of conflict, and all accounts of the old days reveal constant legal disputes often lasting for years. There are many ways of settling legal differences, but the Tlingit selected the indemnity as equal in importance to blood vengeance. The goods used in payment were not destroyed but were set aside for potlatch goods, bride gifts, and the settlement of future disputes. Seldom, if ever, did the Tlingit use this wealth for the satisfaction of his economic needs.

In this chapter I have described the ways in which the Tlingit uses his wealth. We already know how it is produced and through what mechanisms it is distributed. Ostensibly the use of wealth is for the purpose of nourishing the body, for keeping it warm, and for providing it with shelter. But wealth has far wider functions in Tlingit society. It is difficult to say at times which is more important, its purely economic functions or its social functions. Wealth is the product of human effort and like human effort it cannot be said to provide economic security alone. Wealth is used as much in making war as in making peace. In the house-group it serves the need of the body for sustenance as shown in household consumption. There it is collectively produced and collectively consumed, need being the arbiter of distribution.

In the bride gift wealth is as much a means of sexual companionship and the propagation of the race at it is a means for attaining social position for one's self and offspring or for overcoming a rival in the quest for a mate.

In the indemnity wealth functions as a means for settling disputes, in bringing about accord in the relations between individuals and clans. The law of the Tlingit centers around the settlement of wrongs by wealth.

The potlatch is the important enterprise of Tlingit life. Through it a man becomes famous; through it he smashes his rivals; through it he makes his best friends and worst enemies. Through the potlatch a man consolidates his clan or helps break it down. And all this is done with wealth. Therefore, how can one speak of wealth as serving purely economic ends? Among the Tlingit wealth is a means used in attaining all the conflicting ends set up by their society.

APPENDIX

NATURAL RESOURCES
OF THE TLINGIT

Land Animals

Deer (g̣oakaˀn)
Mountain goat (taˀwe)
Mountain sheep (šanawu)
Elk (wats·ix̣)
Caribou (wats·ix̣)
Moose (tsiskʷ)
Porcupine (kaƛagatš)
Marmot (tsax̣)
Squirrel (tsatk)
Coon (g̣analsaˀk)
Muskrat (tsin)
Wolf (quˀtš)
Black bear (siˀk)
Brown bear (hu·ts)
Polar bear (ƛet hu·ts)
Fox (nakasi)
Wolverine (nusk)
Land otter (kušta)
Mink (ƛłukšiaˀn)
Beaver (sik'eti)
Marten (kuh)
Lynx (g̣aˀk)
Rabbit (g̣ax̣)
Weasel (taˀ)

Birds

Duck (g̣aux̣)
Mallard duck (kindašunet)
Squaw duck (g̣aˀx̣)
Goose (taˀuwah)
Swan (k'okutt)
Grouse (nukt)
Ptarmigan (x̣etsawˀa)
Teal (atsk)
Crane (tak a)
Sea gull (keƛte)
Shag (yoˀk)
Eagle (jaˀk)
Raven (yeł)
Crow (tsakwet)

Fish

King salmon ('tah)
Silver salmon (ƛuk)
Sockeye salmon (g̣aˀt)
Humpback salmon (šaˀs)
Dog salmon (tiˀƛ)
Trout (quat h)
Steelhead (aˀšat)

Blueback salmon (ƛukoʔa)
Halibut (tšaʔƛ)
Cod (saʔk)
Tom cod (iškin)
Herring (yawa)
Eulachon (saʔk)
Red snapper (ƛeikʼʷ)

Shellfish

Horse clam (yʌs)
Cockle (yeƛƛuƛet)
Clam (gaʔtˑ)
Small clam (tsikʷ)
Small horse clam (kalkatsk)
Mussel (yaʔk)
Abalone (gunx̣a)
Gum boot (ʔšaʔwa)
   (?) (kuʔu)

Sea Mammals

Whale (yaʔʼ)
Killer-whale (kit)
Porpoise (tšiʔtš)
Big porpoise (gaʔn)
Sea otter (yux̣tš)
White porpoise (ƛiʔtwa)
Hair seal (tsah)
Fur seal (x̣uʔn)
Sea lion (taʔn)

Bushes (berry)

High bush cranberry (x̣akheiq-
   watsi)
Low bush cranberry (x̣aška-
   haku)
Mountain cranberry (tinx̣)
Soapberry (hutx̣ewatsi)
Salmonberry (łekwatsi)
Low bush huckleberry (x̣iʔƛ)

Mountain berry (tsuk ewakʌ)
Serviceberry (kawak)
Elderberry (yiʔƛ)
Blue currant (nistʌyi)
Black currant (šax̣)
Lagoon berry (neguʔn)
Thimbleberry (tšex̣)
Duckberry (takʷ)
Pigeonberry (x̣eł taktša ši)
Raspberry (łakweti)
Jacob berry (kex̣ašaƛ)
Nettleberry (x̣ax̣iyuƛeko)
Redberry(?) (slakiʔbayołeho)

Swampberry(?) $\begin{cases} \text{(nux̣)} \\ \text{(x̣iʔtahan)} \\ \text{(tiłkuhiʔhi)} \\ \text{(łakwetʼi)} \end{cases}$

Trees

Spruce (aʔs)
Cottonwood (tok)
Hemlock (yan)
Yellow cedar (x̣ai)
Willow (x̣iʔšiš)
Crab apple (kax̣watsʌ)
Birch (ʔatʔaʔyi)
Jack pine (łał tšats ʼkaʔasʔi)
Red cedar (łax̣)
Alder (ceˑkʷ)
Maple (kalx̣ʌ)

Roots, Stems, and Seeds

Wild celery (yaʔna)
Wild rhubarb (łagwatš)
Wild rice (x̣uʔh)
Algae (kułʌat)
Seaweed (gaʔtš)
   ? (staʔts)

Medicinal Herbs

Devil's club. The white pulp between the outer green bark and the stem is of medicinal value. When it is chewed it acts as a laxative. It is also taken for venereal disease and can be applied to cuts. When the bark is burned in the house it purifies the air of disease. When branches are placed over the door they keep out disease. Roots and pulp put in bath water are good for rheumatism.

Red berry. Roots are used. When boiled the berry gives a juice that is good for dysentery. Medicine is called kakʔatusaknuk.

X̱ahin root. Roots are boiled, then mashed and diluted with water. This medicine is taken three times a day for tuberculosis.

Klatšaneʔt (mountain ash). Inner bark cooked. Purple liquid produced is very best medicine for tuberculosis and severe colds.

Skunk cabbage. Leaves and roots dried and powered, and mixed with water for headaches and rheumatic pains.

Sax̱ax̱nak(?). Powdered leaf used for poultices, good for cuts and bruises.

Raspberry leaf. Powdered and mixed with pitch and mixed with eagle down. Used as a poultice for flesh wounds.

TLINGIT CLANS

Raven Clans

Most important

1. Ganax̱tedi (people of Ganax); crests: woodworm, frog, black-skinned heron, and the Mother Basket
2. Kiksadi (people of the island of Kiks); crests: frog, goose, owl, sea lion cry
3. Qatšadi (people of Qatš creek on Admiralty Island)
4. Kasqʔaqwedi (camp called Kasqʔe); crests: eagle crane, raven beak, green paint
5. Lenedi (big dipper); crests: dog salmon names
6. Kosk'edi (people of Kosex); crest: mouse
7. Tluk'nax̱adi (king salmon people); crests: king salmon, swan, sleep spirit

8. Tluqaxadi (quick people); crests: real ravens
9. Kask'egoan (people of Kask' creek)

Less important

10. Tenedi (bark house people)
11. K'uxinedi (marten people); crest: whale
12. Takuanedi (winter people); crest: black-skinned heron
13. Saqutenedi (grass people)
14. Tanedi (people of Tan creek); crest: land otter
15. Q'atlšanedi (people of Q'atlšan creek)
16. Kuyedi (people of Kuiu)
17. Tihitan (bark house people); crest: winter raven
18. Tatqoedi (people of Tatqo); crest: a certain mountain
19. Dešitan (people of the end of the road house); crest: beaver
20. Togyedi (outlet people)
21. Anq'akitan (people of the middle of the valley)
22. Taqdentan (retaining timber house); crests: whale, mountain at Cape Fairweather
23. Taqhittan (slug house)—part of the above house
24. Watanedi (part of Kiksadi)
25. Q'at'ka·yi (island people); crests: king salmon, sleep spirit
26. Nušeka·yi (back of fort people)
27. Staxadi ?

Wolf Clans (Wolf in the south, Eagle in the north)

Most important

1. Teqoedi (people of the island of Teqo); crest: grizzly bear
2. Naniyaya (?); crests: grizzly bear, mountain goat head, shark
3. Tšukanedi (bush people) (of low caste); crest: porpoise
4. Kagwantan (burnt house people); crests: wolf, tc'it, murrelet, eagle, grizzly bear, killer-whale
5. Daklawedi (?); crests: murrelet, eagle, killer-whale

Less important

6. Šinkukedi
7. Tlqoayedi

8. Qaq'o'sit·an (human foot house people)
9. Tsaquedi (seal people); crest: killer whale
10. Nesadi (salt water people)
11. Wašinedi (people of the river Was)
12. Nastedi (people of Nass); crest: big rock near Kuiu
13. S'it'qoedi (?); crest: whale
14. S'iknaxadi (?); crest: cane carved like a man
15. Kayasidetan (shelf people)
16. Xełgoan (foam people)
17. Yenedi (hemlock place people); crest: wolf
18. Tsatʔenyedi
19. Wuškitan (?); crest: killer-whale
20. Kukhit·an (part of the Kagwantan)
21. Q'aq'ahit·an (part of the Kagwantan)
22. Katagwedi
23. Taqestina (?); crest: thunder

The petrel was used for a crest by both phratries.

Nexadi: People belonging to neither Raven nor Wolf phratry.

BIBLIOGRAPHY

References Cited

Bancroft, Hubert H. 1886. *History of Alaska*. San Francisco: A. L. Bancroft and Co.

Boas, Franz. 1895. "Report on the North Western Tribes of Canada." Meeting of the British Association for the Advancement of Science, 10th Report. London.

————. 1917. *Grammatical Notes on the Language of the Tlingit*. Philadelphia: University of Pennsylvania Museum.

Durlach, Theresa. 1928. *The Relationship Systems of the Tlingit, Haida, and the Tsimshean*. New York: American Ethnological Society.

Emmons, George T. 1916. *The Whale House of the Chilcat*. Anthropological Papers of the American Museum of Natural History. Vol. 3, part I. New York.

Krause, Aurel. 1885. *Die Tlingit Indianer*. Trans. by Erna Gunther, *The Tlingit Indians*. Seattle: University of Washington Press. 1956.

Swanton, John Reed. 1908. "Social Conditions, Beliefs, and Linguistic Relationships of the Tlingit Indians." Bureau of American Ethnology, 26th Annual Report. Washington, D.C.

————. 1909. *Tlingit Myths and Texts*. Bureau of American Ethnology, Bulletin 39. Washington, D.C.

Some Important Studies of the Tlingit Since 1937

de Laguna, Frederica. 1952. "Some Dynamic Forces in Tlingit Society" *Southwestern Journal of Anthropology* 8:1–12.

————. 1960. *The Story of a Tlingit Community*. Bureau of American Ethnology, Bulletin 172. Washington, D.C.

Based on archaeological and ethnographic field work in 1949 and 1950, this report concentrates on the Angoon area and its people. The archaeological data are supplemented by historical records and ethnographic field information.

Drucker, Philip. 1958. *The Native Brotherhoods*. Bureau of American Ethnology, Bulletin 168. Washington, D.C.

The Alaska Native Brotherhood, which has been a Tlingit-dominated organization since its founding in 1912, is the subject matter for half of this study. The second half of the volume is devoted to a similar organization in British Columbia. Drucker's largely historical study is a highly significant contribution since it is devoted to one of the organized efforts by the Tlingit to promote assimilation into white Alaskan society.

————. 1955. "Sources of Northwest Coast Culture." Pp. 59–81 in *New Interpretations of Aboriginal American Culture History*, edited by Clifford Evans and Betty Meggers. Anthropological Society of Washington, D.C.

Goldschmidt, Walter R., and Theodore H. Haas. 1946. "Possessory Rights of the Natives of Southeastern Alaska." Report to the Commissioner of Indian Affairs (mimeographed).

Keithahn, Edward L. 1963. *Monuments in Cedar*. Rev. ed. Seattle: Superior Publishing Company.

This study is particularly useful in any attempt to trace the origins, antiquity, and development of various forms of totem poles.

McClellan, Catharine. 1954. "The Interrelations of Social Structure with Northern Tlingit Ceremonialism." *Southwestern Journal of Anthropology* 10:75–96.

Ray, Charles K., et al. 1962. *Alaskan Native Secondary School Dropouts*. University of Alaska.

The report in this volume by Seymour Parker on the Tlingit at Hoonah is brief but very good. Parker spent only about a month at Hoonah in 1961, and his emphasis was on values, but considerable additional information is included which is the most up-to-date information in print.

Wardell, Allen, comp. *Yakutat South*. Chicago. 1964.

INDEX

Adultery: ignored within clan, 41; penalty for, 49, 130-31
Adze, 8
Alaska: purchase of, 5
Aleuts, 105
Algae: as part of diet, 8
Amulets, 20, 65
Animals: major types of, hunted and trapped, 8; conventionalized rendering of, in art, 14; as crests, 43-44; imitated in dances, 16. *See also names of specific animals*
Ankaua ("rich man"), 42-43
Anyeti ("noble class"), 41, 42, 61, 87
Athapascans: intermarriage with, 7; trade with, 9, 108, 110; mentioned, 56, 103, 106

Baranov, Aleksandr Andreevich, 5
Baskets: Mother Basket, 43; weaving of, as female activity, 85; use of, in trade, 107; mentioned, 9, 72
Batons, 13, 16, 120
Bear; 67, 71, 111
Berries: major types of, 8; ownership of patches, 55, 59; storage of, 71, 74; season for picking and storage, 74, 77; picking of, as joint male and female activity, 86
Birds: major types of, hunted, 8; conventionalized rendering of, in art, 14; as crests, 43-44. *See also* Raven
Birth: rites and customs connected with, 21-22, 38, 53, 84, 95

Blankets: weaving of, as female activity, 85; gifts of, at potlatch, 118, 119, 120, 124. *See also* Chilcat blanket
Boas, Franz, 6, 7, 12
Boxes, 9, 62, 94
Bride price: as determiner of rank, 35, 131; use of surplus food for, 103, discussed, 129-30; mentioned, 22, 33, 55, 101, 125
Burial. *See* Funeral rites

Canneries, 5
Canoes: two types of, 9; construction of, described, 9; collective production and use of, 30, 62, 80, 102; amulets placed in, 65; use of, for hunting, 68, 71; obtained from Haida and Tsimshian, 70, 109; carving of, as specialized work, 84; production of, as male activity, 85; as gifts, 94; mentioned, 10, 73, 89
Carving: increasing importance of, 84-85
Chilcat blanket: described, 15; importance of, for trade; 70, 107; worn on ceremonial occasions, 116, 119; mentioned, 13, 14, 108
Chisel, 8
Clan: as political unit, 23; matrilineal, 23, 63; importance of local division of, 39, 55; functions of, at potlach, 40, 124; local division's ownership of salmon streams and hunting grounds, 40, 55, 56, 71; re-